MANAGIN(
IN THE I
AND CA1 _.... ⌐u
INDUSTRY

Steven Goss-Turner

Croner Publications Limited
Croner House
London Road
Kingston upon Thames
Surrey KT2 6SR
Telephone: 081-547 3333

Copyright © 1992 S. Goss-Turner
First published 1992

Published by
Croner Publications Ltd
Croner House
London Road
Kingston upon Thames
Surrey KT2 6SR
Telephone: 081-547 3333

British Library Cataloguing in Publication Data
A CIP Catalogue Record for this book
is available from the British Library.

ISBN 1-85524-102-1

-

Phototypeset by Avonset, Midsomer Norton, Bath, England
Printed by Whitstable Litho Ltd, Whitstable, Kent

MANAGING PEOPLE IN THE
HOTEL AND CATERING INDUSTRY

To Beryl, John and Gang

ACKNOWLEDGEMENTS

It is indicative of the overall spirit within the hospitality industry that so many people were of great help to me in the writing of this book. In particular I would like to thank the following for their information and advice: Sarah Chater, Debbie Donnelly, Alison Curtis, Robin Marrow, John and Julie Foley, Janice Close, Peter Jones and all my colleagues at Brighton Polytechnic.

CONTENTS

Part 2 continued

Part 3 – Issues at Work 135

INTRODUCTION

The people who work in the hotel and catering industry are to be found in many thousands of very different locations throughout the country. They form a workforce, 2.5 million strong, of vital importance to the British economy, an economy to which tourism as a whole was worth over £8000 million in 1990 according to the British Hospitality Association. Whether they work in large city centre hotels or small country inns, in fashionable restaurants or in industrial catering units, their ultimate aim is service. Such an objective demands that the "people-element" is crucial. The business of providing hospitality is labour intensive and its success depends fundamentally on the skills and commitment of the employees in the front line. And it is estimated that one in ten Europeans now works in this "hospitality" industry.

Yet the function of personnel management has often been viewed as a necessary evil, an expense created by the socially conscious with no concern for profitability and business growth. More enlightened management clearly sees the *human resource* (HR) very differently. Employees are at last being seen as a true resource, as valuable as any financial asset, and needing to be managed just as carefully and intelligently. Expenditure on personnel and training must be considered no longer as an avoidable cost, but as a shrewd investment, the return on which will be sustained commercial success.

THE PURPOSE OF THIS BOOK

The hotel and catering industry is still rapidly developing its approach to the many real problems and issues which its human resources management (HRM) faces. The image, and too often the fact, is one of a desperate shortage of technical and interpersonal skills, unacceptably high labour turnover and a lack of effective training methods. Industry leaders are aware of the need to change radically the perception of the hotel, catering and leisure business as an employer. Terms and conditions will always need to be more and more competitive and attractive. And underpinning all these issues is the very nature of a service industry; the everyday difficulties which arise from a high pressure business, totally dependent on a series of task-based interpersonal and skill relationships. To ensure that just one meal is served to just one happy customer may take the successful management and interface of up to eleven different and specialist employees. One break in that human resource chain threatens the business.

This handbook addresses the handling of these everyday "people difficulties". Essentially it is a practical guide, advising hospitality managers and supervisors on the most effective ways to overcome their key human resource (HR) challenges. The purpose is to complement all the legal and procedural reference material and advice that is available with "best practice" hints on how to deal with the problem, very often in a face-to-face situation. The book is therefore behavioural in its bias, considering the application of knowledge and information.

My respect for the pressure on hospitality people in terms of both time and sheer workload, has driven me to produce the material in a format designed for easy, quick reference. In this way readers may use the book every day in order to obtain one or two pointers on a specific issue. The purpose is also to convey one of my own beliefs: that personnel management is not a constant stream of traumatic incidents, but is fun, rewarding and satisfying, and a key contribution to the quality of life debate. I hope that suggestions and guidance in this book will help readers to discover and realise the many benefits of effective people management.

THE READERSHIP

At first glance, the book may seem appropriate for personnel managers only. Clearly, those involved in management responsible specifically for employees are a prime target audience, but managing people is a component part of every supervisor's and line manager's job. Their objectives can only be reached through their staff. The issues raised in this handbook are therefore of importance to both specialist and generalist managers.

In companies and enterprises of different sizes, the level of personnel management varies dramatically. An hotel with 650 employees may need a full time HR function, numbering five or six specialists. A medium-sized restaurant complex with 40 on the staff will probably delegate the personnel duties to an assistant manager who is very much an operator most of the time. The degree of support and advice therefore differs with the size of the business and whether or not there is a corporate resource available. This book will be of use to all these individuals, and especially the many independent businesses or the smaller groups, without the back-up of large head offices. Students and trainees should also find the material useful in illustrating the practical application of their more theoretical education.

THE FORMAT

The text is presented in four sections.

1. The Human Resource Manager's Role
2. The Employment Process
3. Issues at Work
4. External Relations

Each section covers many specific topics which are alphabetically indexed for speedy reference. The emphasis is on a step-by-step treatment with clear and concise "bullet points" to supplement the ammunition readers may already possess.

The Human Resource Manager's Role examines the overall concepts of an HR function, whether full time or not, and how it can contribute more significantly to business success.

The Employment Process considers the many aspects affecting management throughout the recruitment process, from deciding that a vacancy really does exist, to on-the-job training of a new employee.

Issues at Work reflects the enormous scope of human resource management, touching on a number of potent topics confronting the hotel and catering industry and its workforce.

External Relations stresses that any business is not an insular enterprise, but is a most important part of the local and national economy. Such a business can only prosper by developing a culture of collaboration and cooperation.

USING THE BOOK

The format of the book is such that apart from reading the text as a whole, it is possible to be extremely selective and use it at the moment demanded by a certain situation or development. All too often, management needs to ask itself, "How should I actually handle this issue; what should or should I not say?". Legal information is readily available, and larger companies may have a procedural manual or advice service. Reference to such literature is vital in establishing the letter of the law or the agreed company policy. Yet it is necessary to face the behavioural application, in the office, with the individual, when written procedures seem so far away. This handbook should be used in conjunction with legal guides, text books and company instructions, to assist in concluding a constructive and successful human resource encounter.

I am sure readers will come across situations not covered in the book. After all, people management is like that – unpredictably exciting, never predictably dull. I would be delighted to hear of such additional issues, through the publisher, so that this handbook becomes even more relevant in the future.

Part 1
THE HUMAN RESOURCE MANAGER'S ROLE

COMPETITIVE EDGE

The hotel and catering industry is increasingly competitive, across every sector from high street fast food outlets to in-vogue restaurants and country house hotels. The decade ahead will only strengthen this trend. International companies see the entire globe as their potential market and a Europe with reduced trading restrictions will be a major battleground of commercial warfare. The management of people must be fully integrated into any business strategy as a formidable weapon in ensuring victory over the competition. Customers will return again and again if employees give them outstanding service matched to a quality product and value for money. It is the staff that give the "added value". Hotels in city centres, for example, will often have a very similar physical product, from private bathrooms to hair dryers, trouser presses and a business centre. It is the human element which gives the crucial edge that achieves success for one hotel over another.

Personnel and training: investment not cost

This concept takes us back to the principle that the personnel and training function is an investment not a cost. This fact is now endorsed by the Government, which has launched a new award for industry. To qualify for the "Investors in People" kitemark, companies need to satisfy a range of criteria, including the inclusion of training in their business plan, and the review of human resource activities at board level. Directors, managers and all in positions of influence need to be totally convinced that professional strategic personnel management gives their business real competitive advantages and maximises profitability.

At unit level, whatever the size, it is necessary to consider the *local* competition. The surrounding community forms the potential workforce and customers. The standing and respect of a business within that community can be a vital issue. At the local level it means that the business:

(a) is the first choice for potential staff
(b) gets the best staff
(c) keeps them
(d) gives the best training
(e) attains appropriate and consistent standards for staff and customers
(f) customers return.

These targets must never be far from the mind. Maintaining competitive advantage is as tough as gaining it in the first place. It is necessary to be constantly thinking about the business and its people, never accepting the *status quo*, no matter how currently successful it is.

Existing arrangements should be questioned, some aspects should be improved and innovation must be directed towards others. Creativity is as important in human resource management (HRM) as in design. In the competitive labour market it is necessary particularly to consider:

(a) terms and conditions
(b) incentives and recognition
(c) benefits
(d) the working environment
(e) recruitment campaigns
(f) selection methods
(g) training methods
(h) staff consultation.

All these topics should be embraced by an appropriate management style. Investment in a resource called people will encourage and inspire that resource. If people *want* to work for a business, it really has secured a potent competitive edge.

EVALUATION

There is only one catch connected to the view that human resource management (HRM) must be seen as an investment : a return will be expected. Only then will HRM be fully integrated and accepted as an inseparable feature of business strategy and performance. It is necessary to be able to provide hard evidence and outcomes to illustrate that these activities really do pay, in hard currency terms wherever possible. This is not easy. A sales executive can report back the number of sales calls made, the number converted to confirmed sales and the comparison of business gained against targets. But converting a training course into hard currency benefits is not so straightforward. How is it possible to evaluate the benefit of a first rate induction of a new employee? How is it possible to prove that a customer care training programme really increased average spend in the coffee shop? Perhaps the chef improved the product at the same time. And when absenteeism levels are reduced, does the management realise the true benefit of every single day saved?

Measurable criteria

For too long, personnel practitioners have talked in terms of "long term benefit — impossible to put a figure on it". In certain areas, there is some truth in the statement. But in many areas it is possible to be more analytical, using measurable criteria: measure performance against targets and budgets, and convert hidden costs such as accidents and labour turnover into hard figures — the only measurement which is convincing to many operators. The lack of specific data to support and evaluate human resource activities has only helped to promote the opinion that these areas are a vague and expensive luxury with no tangible benefit to the profit and loss account, no real return on the investment.

Any person responsible for the people element of a business must be ready and able to prove the worth of managing and training employees more effectively. So what follows is a checklist of aspects which *can* be measured and compared, thus confirming concern about the success of the business. When considering the ideas and suggestions below, ask the following questions:

(a) Have I got the relevant data?
(b) How can I get it?
(c) Can I compare figures year on year?
(d) What targets can I set?
(e) What factors will influence future performance?
(f) Which areas will most benefit the business plan?

Further information on the topics listed below can be found within this book by referring to the Contents and Index.

- Absenteeism rates
- Sickness rates of absence
- Accidents index   — Include days lost and cost
- Inductions completed
- Trainees in post
- Training courses   — Completed and planned
  - Number of delegates
  - Percentage attendance
  - Benefits, financial if possible against original objective

- Training qualifications gained
- Appraisals completed
- Number of internal promotions
- Recruitment cost reduction
- Productivity levels   — Performance against norms
- Performance evaluations   — Sales per employee
  - Profit per employee
  - Wages percentage to sales
  - Wages budget forecast v actual
- Competition successes   — eg Hotelympia
  - Salon culinaires
  - Local events
  - Publicity benefits
- Incentive programmes   — Financial benefits
- Staff attitude surveys
- Grievances reduction
- Disciplinaries reduction
- College and school visits
- Labour turnover   — Annual % rate:

$$\frac{\text{Number of leavers during period}}{\text{Average number employed}} \times 100$$

     — Stability index:

$$\frac{\text{Number with more than 1 year's service}}{\text{Total employed 1 year ago}} \times 100$$

     — Total cost of losing 1 employee estimated at £700.

HUMAN RESOURCE MANAGEMENT

Imported phrases and jargon from the United States, for example, referring to the financial loss of a business as "negative profit" or calling redundancy an "alternative career development enhancement programme", often obscure the real issues! However, the term human resources (HR) which did come from the USA, is a concise and accurate description of what is so often termed personnel and training or staff management. It correctly indicates the true strategic significance of the function, portraying a professional and business-conscious approach to the management of people.

Human resource management, increasingly abbreviated to HRM, is a most appropriate concept and title in the business environment of today. It is an important development, indeed an evolution, for the standing, status and contribution of the discipline within commercial enterprises. Evolution is an appropriate word because any form of personnel management is in a very early stage of its development. If other disciplines such as banking, accounting and law have histories dating back many centuries, then personnel management is only in its first century of growth.

Born within altruistic, well-meaning employers of the 19th century, personnel management functions developed through the vehicle of welfare in mainly manufacturing companies in the early 20th century. Those industries based on production and assembly lines, were greatly influenced by management theorists of the day and soon realised the advantage of properly directing the ever greater and more concentrated factory workforces. The approach became "scientific", with skills such as work study to the fore. Later the human relations schools of more enlightened industrial psychologists orchestrated a total rethink of the needs and aspirations of people at work.

The economy today

The make-up of our economy today is one where manufacturing and heavy industry have declined sharply and the service industries, hospitality included, have assumed significant dominance. Many local economies are based heavily on service. In Sussex, for example, nearly 68 per cent of businesses are service industries, 22 per cent are manufacturing and 10 per cent are professions. Service industry is highly labour-intensive, and often succeeds or falls by the quality of its employees. So, highly professional management of the human resource is crucial. Yet the development of effective human resource management in the hospitality industry has been slow, some might say snail-like, and only recently have firms and individual operators begun to give it the importance it really warrants. At last, enlightened employers have raised the emphasis until human resources are of strategic importance in their organisational structures and business plans.

HRM should be seen as a development in philosophy from the traditional ideas of "staff management". It demands that people are considered as a key resource or asset to a business. In the past great care would always be taken over the capital outlay on a new piece of equipment, perhaps an oven or a new computer but little care was taken over a new employee. In the past personnel and training managers jumped when line management called; they were reactive and obedient. Now, human resource specialists need to be proactive, assessing the needs of business and workforce, and presenting operators with the up-to-date issues, trends, information and proposals upon which they can make better decisions. HRM demands that decisions are affected by the human resource team, not just accepted by them.

The role of human resource management

The role of HR managers must be to identify strongly with the interests of the business, as well as those of the employees. This means getting off the comfortable fence. Only profitable, growing businesses can continue to support their employees, providing better working terms and conditions. It is necessary to be fully aware of business plans and objectives, and be responsive to changes. HR managers should aim at the successful integration of the needs of the business and the needs of the staff, constantly assessing and anticipating the effect that strategic and tactical decisions will have on the people of the business. HR managers are thus motivators of vital resources, as influential as any operations or other specialist function.

The status of human resource management

The status of personnel management within the hospitality industry has only been elevated in recent times. Even job titles illustrated the perceived relevance of the area. Management teams often consisted of

General Manager, Food and Beverage Manager, Chief Accountant, Sales and Marketing Director, and there would be a Personnel Officer, a sort of "clerk of works" installed in an unimpressive office. Today this scenario is changing. Human resource managers and their departments are increasingly recognised as a showcase for potential labour, an adjunct to the entire marketing plan of the business. The new role is that of a professional manager fully integrated into the management team.

Example

In discussion with the Food and Beverage Manager, an hotel Personnel Manager reviewed the poor performance of the coffee shop operation, in particular a high number of customer complaints, received both verbally and by customer feedback questionnaire. Below is an extract from the Action Plan devised by the Personnel Manager, the original of which contained time plan and success criteria.

1. Analyse coffee shop financial results and content of customer complaints.
2. Refer to Food and Beverage business plan to establish agreed plans for the outlet and overall direction of hotel's catering.
3. Analyse complaints for people-related problems.
4. Audit and review entire staffing structure of coffee shop, including management and supervision.
5. Review training methods, including departmental induction, on-the-job training and update training.
6. Establish with Food and Beverage Manager the agreed standards and service delivery systems.
7. Prepare plan as follows and present to Food and Beverage Manager and General Manager:

The Plan

- Coffee Shop standards to undergo total review and clarification.
- All supervisors to be assessed for managerial and training skills.

- All staff to be assessed for technical abilities, product knowledge and interpersonal skills.
- Training programme to implement agreed standards and service strategy.
- Training programme for supervisors in new order and billing computer system, already planned in Food and Beverage Business Plan.
- Incentive scheme for staff to be introduced, as highlighted in Hotel Business Plan, to be based on proficiency testing following staff training.
- New uniforms and name badges to be introduced.
- Evaluation of the Plan to be based on specified reduction in complaints, incidence of repeat customers and increased average spend.

This plan illustrates the need to view human resources within the total business; it is not an isolated item or merely a method of reacting by "fire fighting" and "putting on another training course". Operational matters such as standards should be questioned just as much as staffing levels and training activity. It is a package of measures, not a piecemeal lesson in crisis management. It also sets targets and reasonable objectives so that evaluation can be undertaken and tangible results presented to senior management.

HUMAN RESOURCE PLANNING

When I was a somewhat inexperienced personnel manager of an hotel in the late 1970s, I was constantly amazed at the unacceptable demands of other line managers and heads of departments. They always needed more staff, almost immediately, and stood before me expecting me to produce instant, almost magical, results. "I need three more for the function on Saturday" requested the Banqueting Manager. "I'll need another in the bar tonight", stated the Head Barman, whilst the Head Housekeeper, seated with clipboard in hand, highlighted sections not covered for the next two weeks. Whilst naturally showing caring concern, I often wondered to myself how these people got in such a mess. I never thought it was my fault or considered that with more systematic planning, intelligent anticipation and some experienced forethought, I could have assisted line management and myself by drastically reducing the "last minute panic" so often associated with staffing.

There will always be unplanned events in the hospitality industry and management will need to react accordingly. But so many factors can be planned for and assessed in a proactive fashion, anticipating needs and business demands so as to ensure continued quality and success in the delivery of service.

This section examines the issues which can be considered when planning human resource activities over a future period of time. Human resource planning should correlate with business planning, normally on an annual basis, and must take into account many local and national trends and factors. In this way we can get away from many "fire-fighting" nightmares often experienced by personnel management and line management alike. If the human resource truly is an integral feature of business success, then it must be approached on a professional basis, with planning as a key element. Proactive management planning minimises the chaos and begins to ensure that the competitive edge is maintained through optimum staffing levels and optimum wage costs to sales revenue, whilst assuring the provision of an agreed quality in product and service.

A plan

When formulating a human resource plan for an outlet, whatever the size, whatever the sector of the industry, the questions below should lead to information which can greatly influence the business' future activities and priorities. Assess the answers on their potential impact on personnel, such as number required, specific skills needed and the training necessary, and always ensure that plans are in direct support of the wider business plan for the unit and company. Examples of influencing factors are given for each question.

Question	Example factors
What national factors could influence the plan?	National economy
	Regional economy
	Government initiatives on employment and training
	Industrial relations
	Demographics
	Legislation, eg Food Safety Act

9

Question	Example factors
Which aspects of the business plan need to be considered?	Significant changes Expansion Menu changes Change in style of service Refurbishment schemes Product change Organisation structure The customer Market mix change New restaurant Weekly/monthly/annual business patterns
What is the annual business profile?	Seasonal peaks/troughs Special events Special promotions Major conferences in town Local festivals Bi-annual events, eg Farnborough Air Show
When are the predictably significant dates for planning? Also, when can staff be encouraged to take holiday and time off?	Christmas Easter All Bank Holidays Job fairs Careers conventions Trainee placements
What are the local competition factors?	New hospitality outlets Refurbishment plans Changes in style Recruitment campaigns Terms and conditions offered Provision of accommodation Skills competitors

Question	Example factors
What new technology is to be introduced?	Front office systems Accounting systems Ordering/billing systems New equipment New office systems Business centre opening Leisure centre upgrade
Which personnel changes can be anticipated?	Succession plans Retirals Management moves Appraisal results Long service staff Labour turnover patterns Individuals' performance
What recruitment will be necessary?	Numbers Types and skills Experience required Internal promotions Company trainees Company transfers Campaign necessary? Source of recruits When will we recruit?
What training can be planned?	Legal — fire training Health and safety First aid Inductions New skills and knowledge Refresher training Customer care campaign Training the trainers Trainees

Question	Example factors
With whom must we keep in touch?	Schools, colleges
	Local authority
	Local trade associations
	Job Centre
	Head office
	Former employees
	Recruitment agencies
	Wage control personnel
How can we ensure that other line managers and supervisors also *plan*?	Commitment of boss
	Business forecasts
	Rotoring to business
	Weekly department plan
	Wages forecasts
	Review timesheets
	Overtime and casuals

IMAGE

Hospitality managers have long been concerned with their public image and it is important to be seen in the correct light. All too often this perfectly sensible consciousness over image has not included their image as an employer. Perhaps in bygone days of "hire and fire" such an image was immaterial. In the fierce marketplace of today, the highly competitive objective of getting and keeping the best staff available demands that employers of every size address this fundamental question of workforce public relations. Every interaction and transaction with a potential employee, regardless of position and seniority, is an opportunity to establish and reinforce the business' standing as an employer. Fortunately, today many firms and businesses are smartening up their act, attempting to leave far behind the following catalogue of events related by a candidate considering a position in a three-star hotel in the Midlands, in 1991.

Experience no. 1:   Told by off-hand hall porter to go round the back to the staff entrance.

Experience no. 2:   Back door timekeeper instructs that "You go to personnel", gesturing in the general direction with a sandwich.

Experience no. 3:	Eventually finds the basement retreat with dilapidated decor and furniture.
Experience no. 4:	Brusque, disinterested girl hands seven-page application form to candidate: "You fill that in".
Experience no. 5:	Candidate, standing, attempts to complete application form against wall, as chair is broken.
Experience no. 6:	Duty Manager tries to help and moves applicant to busiest public area in the hotel.

This is the type of scenario which does untold harm to the public image of the hospitality industry as an employer, and it is especially galling as so many managers are striving hard to reduce this often out-of-date impression.

Those who have contact with existing and potential employees must be fully aware of the powerful influence on the labour market of their attitude, behaviour and the physical surroundings. Of course, smaller restaurants and hotels cannot have dedicated personnel offices, but however and wherever potential employees are handled must convey the most professional image possible.

Guidelines for image improvement

- Train existing staff in how to handle and direct potential employees and their enquiries.
- Ensure that if a personnel office exists, it is smart, tidy and comfortable.
- Ensure that any office where interviewing takes place projects a caring and professional impression.
- Ensure that applicants have a private place to complete the application form and help them if necessary.
- Offer a cup of coffee or tea; after all we are the hospitality industry. Set an example.
- For existing staff, and in larger units, create a wages collection point that is secure but attractive — not a "prison" dispensing hand-outs to the unfortunate.
- Personnel dealing with employees should be smart, socially skilled and genuinely interested. Uniforms could be used in larger outlets.

- Signs, notices and information boards should be updated and attractive.
- All stationery, letter heads and similar items should be well presented, with clear and accurate contents.
- Written or telephone enquiries should be handled efficiently and promptly with quick follow-up to interviews.
- Remember that image is also projected on the telephone, a common means of contact for prospective staff.
- Every applicant, however unlikely, must be treated with professional sensitivity. In the local community the business' image as an employer spreads quickly and sticks permanently.

MARKETING THE HUMAN RESOURCE

It is my experience over the last decade that if one invites any group of delegates on a training course to nominate the firm they believe to be the best employer in the UK, a majority will select Marks and Spencer. This enviable status has clearly been well-earned over a long period of time. It is also a testament to the fact that it really does pay to market and promote a firm's human resource activities. It has often been a proud boast of that company that it never needs to advertise for staff. Such is the power of a good image, backed up by sensible promotions. Those responsible for the human resource in any size of unit, whether a single business or a multi-national organisation, should consider applying some of the basic principles of good marketing to the issue of people.

The market is the potential and existing workforce. These are the people who are the customers, who need to know the product, like it, and be satisfied when they enter into a transaction. The market could be locally based, such as a nearby housing estate or a technical college; it may be national, such as Head Chefs in similar establishments nationwide; it may be in specific locations of high unemployment, markets which can be easily penetrated by job offers linked to accommodation. Wherever the labour force comes from, a business must have the right product — that is, the right package of terms and conditions. Potential employees must be attracted using the most effective media; then they must be satisfied and retained. This subject can be broken down into three subsections and some examples and pointers are given under each heading.

(a) *Marketing within the management team*
- Illustrate the value of good human resources management.
- Convince management and colleagues.
- Be proactive.
- Be involved in the real decision making forums.
- Be conscious of costs and profit.
- Promote good human resource public and press relations.
- Campaign for good human resources management.

(b) *Marketing to existing and potential staff*
- Devise attractive and appropriate packages.
- Ensure that terms and conditions of employment are competitive.
- Treat staff and potential staff as customers.
- Arrange open days/visits for local people.
- Undertake open days/visits for schools and colleges.
- Ensure that advertising copy is professional.
- Ensure that copy projects the required image.
- Get involved in local societies and associations.
- Forge good relations with the Job Centre and other agencies.
- Consider sponsorship involvement in the local community.
- Promote introductory bonuses for staff supplying candidates.

(c) *Marketing yourself*
- Get your own image right.
- Ensure courtesy and helpfulness within your office.
- Agree a certain approach to your customers.
- Consider uniforms, office decor and use of first names.
- Set an example in telephone manner.
- All printed output from the HR office should be professional and accurate.
- Consider print style, letter head, logo standards.
- Agree standards for advertising copy.
- Consider additional media such as a newsletter.
- Be proactive in organising special events for staff, eg, formulate a social calendar, arrange health awareness sessions, and organise sports and recreation teams.

OFFICE ORGANISATION

The level and structure of human resource support and office accommodation will vary greatly from a restaurant employing four full-timers to a major hotel administering a staff of over 600. However, the underlying principles of professionalism and care must be upheld, whether from a single desk in a shared management office, or from a suite of dedicated offices in a self-contained personnel department. Other basic similarities also exist. Regardless of numbers, certain pieces of information and personnel records are necessary for every employee, very often dictated by law. To assist in this aspect of office organisation, Appendix 2 Personnel Records provides examples of the types of pro formas required. Reference may also be made to *Croner's Personnel in Practice* (*see Further reading*) and also *Human Resource Management in the Hospitality Industry* by Michael J. Boella.

General factors which should be considered when reviewing or planning personnel office organisation

- The general standard and quality of appearance of personnel staff, and their demeanour. Give all employees or potential employees the feeling that they can trust personnel people with their employment and personal details.
- Decide on an "open door" policy and other arrangements for staff access.
- Review the physical route to be taken by potential staff during the recruitment process, eg:
  - How will they find the personnel office?
  - Where will they wait to be seen?
  - Where will they complete the application form?
  - Where will they be interviewed?
- Agree with management the arrangements for administrative support.
- Ensure easy access to some private office. Many discussions on people issues will be intensely confidential.
- Consider security matters, eg:
  - wages (collation, storage and distribution points)
  - personal files (locked cabinet)
  - keys (locked key cupboards for accommodation and personal locker keys).

    — filing cabinets (lockable to secure personal files, corres-
      pondence, pro formas, tax forms, etc)
    — desk (secure, especially if used to store personal infor-
      mation)
    — computers (restrict access via a password or other security
      features).

- Consider which forms and documents will be needed frequently and organise them so that they are conveniently to hand.
- Ensure that other members of the management team, especially duty managers for example, are aware of how they can obtain vital documents for themselves.
- Large departments, probably in big hotels, industrial catering units or leisure parks, may consider a computerised system. Clearly a cost/benefit feasibility study would need to be undertaken but many outlets now use such systems for personnel records and word processing. For further information see the next topic in this section, "Personnel Information Systems".
- In larger personnel departments, or where certain human resource activities are delegated to various members of line management, consider a division of responsibilities which the personnel-responsible manager will need to coordinate (see example below).

Example: three-star hotel — 150 employees

Responsibility	Employee Category	Person Responsible
Recruitment	Management and Heads of Department (HODs)	General Manager
Recruitment	Supervisors and staff	Assistant Manager – Personnel and Heads of Department
Administration	All employees	Assistant Manager – Personnel and General Managers Secretary
Induction	All employees	Assistant Manager – Personnel, General Manager and Heads of Department

Responsibility	Employee Category	Person Responsible
Training	Management and Heads of Department	Company Training department, external providers
Training	Supervisors and staff	Management, Heads of Department, on-the-job trainers
Wages administration	All employees	Financial controller and line management
Staff social and welfare	All employees	Assistant Manager – Personnel and General Manager

- Personnel records (see Appendix 2 for pro forma examples). The following list covers a range of possible forms, some of which may be unnecessary within particular organisations.

  Personnel/staff requisition
  Application form
  Internal vacancy application form
  Recruitment progress form
  Interview assessment
  Offer letter
  Health questionnaire
  Food handler's declaration
  Internal notification of engagement
  Statement of terms and conditions
  Personal history record
  Induction checklist
  Itemised pay statement
  Job description
  Activity plan
  Holiday pay and entitlement
  Absence and holiday request
  Sickness self-certification
  Absence record
  Notification of maternity leave
  Maternity leave
  Accident log
  Warning letter
  Notification of termination
  Checklist on termination
  Leaver's form
  Termination interview

PERSONNEL INFORMATION SYSTEMS

A recent survey, *Computers in Personnel*, carried out by the Institute of Manpower Studies carries the following line in its introduction:

> Walk into any personnel department and you are bound to find a computer "whiz kid" who is capable of trading ROMs, RAMs, and Dongles with the best.

This may not necessarily be the case in many hospitality industry personnel departments but computerised personnel information systems have developed rapidly in the last decade in many industries. The pressure to have quick, accurate information in an environment and economy of rapid change is paramount in making the best operational decisions. In hospitality, this sort of development is very much in its infancy, largely confined to very large establishments and corporate head offices. So many of the single businesses involved in hospitality cannot and will not justify considerable expenditure on sophisticated personnel information technology. Manual systems will remain a feature of their human resources administrative support.

Computerisation

Computerisation has largely been confined to key operational functions and specialist support services. Hotel front offices, accounts departments, general catering stock control systems, and restaurant ordering and billing are some common applications in use.

Within the area of personnel, only payroll and pensions have been regularly computerised and then nearly always in the large chains. Yet the personnel function is in many ways a very suitable case for computerisation. A great deal of information and many records need to be kept, increasingly so as employment legislation proliferates. Training records alone are now vital with regard to statutory obligations relating to fire, health, hygiene and safety.

Furthermore, much of the correspondence is of a regular and repetitive nature. Word processing can introduce time-saving efficiency here, with the creation of standard letter frameworks. Offer and regret letters, general enquiry replies and many pro formas, like warning and accident reports, may be stored in the word processor. Many larger hospitality units have invested in word processing installations for their personnel work, although stopping short of the much more expensive fully integrated personnel system.

A high financial outlay is required to acquire a personnel information system: any sensible human resource manager must ask many searching questions before rushing to the management with an enthusiastic but expensive and unconvincing proposal. Above all, it must be shown exactly how the expenditure will benefit the *business* as a whole, not just the personnel department. That means a return in terms of greater efficiency, reduction of costs and increased profitability. The purpose of the personnel information system must be to aid management decision making by the provision of the information needed by line management — accurately, quickly and cost effectively.

Computerisation benefits the human resource manager by enabling proactivity, thus assisting the integration of personnel and the business in the key decision making events. By reducing administration and time-consuming pen-pushing, the human resource manager should be able to spend more time managing people.

To help in deciding whether or not even to think about proposing the "high tech" route, consider the factors below:

The benefits of a personnel information system to the business

It is necessary to review totally the information needs of line management. The system *must* assist management decision making, must improve efficiency, and provide a return on capital invested through reduction of costs. It is often the key to management being *truly* proactive.

How can a personnel information system benefit the human resource function?

Acquiring a splendid new system will not suddenly make a personnel department more efficient. Think clearly about what is required from the system and how it will affect existing methods, organisation and staffing.

What facilities can systems offer?

- Payroll and pensions
- personnel details

- word processing
- recruitment administration
- employment contracts
- appraisal records
- absenteeism rates
- medical records
- training records
- salary and wages analysis
- manpower planning
- manpower budgeting
- succession plans.

The more sophisticated systems will only be considered by company head offices. Most outlets will be interested in word processing, storage of basic personnel details and payroll administration.

Evaluating a system

Choose a retailer, examine the systems available, seek advice and information about prices and compare the features against a user specification. This latter item is a detailed analysis of the work and processes carried out by the department, including the type and amount of information needed by line management.

The Data Protection Act

Under the Data Protection Act 1984, any organisation which keeps personnel records on computer must register as a data user with the Data Protection Registrar, unless the information is only used to compute payroll and pensions. For further details consult *Croner's Catering* or contact the Data Protection Registrar (address in Appendix 3).

YOUR BEHAVIOUR

Behaviour is important in any position of managerial status. Due to the very nature of the interpersonal content of the training and management of people, it is crucial to understand one's own behavioural skills and those of other people. The behaviour of the human resource manager is made significant because of the central and influential role he or she plays, dealing with all the other people in the business in regular interactions.

Interviewing, counselling, training, appraisals, settling personal conflicts – these are all intensely behavioural situations requiring maturity and highly developed interpersonal skills. The manager will make decisions, reach conclusions and take action based on people's behaviour, both non-verbal and verbal. This could determine whether one trusts a colleague, believes in an employee or recommends for selection a candidate just interviewed.

It is necessary for human resource managers to remember that colleagues and other fellow workers will be making decisions, reaching conclusions and taking action from their observations of the managers' behaviour. They will use managers' behaviour to determine whether they can trust them, would come to them for counselling about a personal crisis, or for fair dealing on a grievance.

The human resource manager may be first-rate in his or her knowledge of personnel legislation, be able to fulfil many of the roles required of a personnel specialist and be a brilliant administrator, but if he or she does not possess the vital ingredient of exceptional behavioural skills, he or she cannot be a truly effective manager of a personnel and training function.

As a means of measuring behavioural "performance" to date, managers should use the questions below as the basis for thinking about themselves for a while. They should be honest: self-deception is a pointless activity. It may be a good idea for them to discuss answers with a close colleague and then decide whether to modify some aspects of their own interpersonal skills.

Behavioural performance questions

- What image do I have of myself?
- What image do colleagues have of me?
- What image do staff have of me?
- How do I behave under normal conditions?
- How do I behave in a crisis?
- How do I behave towards customers?
- How do I behave at meetings?
- What personal characteristics do I display?
- How socially skilled am I?

- What motivates me?
- What do I do that makes a specific person behave in a certain way?

As with any profession or industry, there are specifically practical issues which must be addressed. These pertain to the human resource manager's position, influence and the characteristics of the hospitality business. Many of these considerations, a number of which are discussed below, emanate from the manager's role as a guardian of many behavioural standards within the organisation. These standards are initially established during the recruitment and selection process, formalised by contracts of employment and handbooks, house rules, induction and training. The manager responsible for personnel and training is therefore seen by employees as the focal point of such standards of behaviour and performance. This puts a particularly significant responsibility on the job-holder and some of the aspects to consider are noted below.

1. Spoken and unspoken behaviour must reinforce the organisation's standards, setting an example to all other employees. The manager's influence and credibility depend upon it. Aspects to consider include:
   (a) appearance
   (b) image
   (c) positiveness
   (d) a caring approach
   (e) concern with standards
   (f) tone of voice
   (g) listening skills.
2. The human resource manager must set an example in personal activities and conduct. For example, if employees see him or her drinking on duty, what authority will he or she have when required to discipline a member of staff on an issue of misconduct?
3. Behaviour is easily mirrored by subordinates. An aggressive and off-hand manner with customers or staff will seriously endanger the business because it sets a standard others may follow.
4. An over-friendly approach to employees can be just as dangerous. The manager's approach can be socially skilled, but must always be totally professional. Otherwise discipline and his or her role could be severely compromised.

5. Care should be taken not to appear to have favourites or display personal bias or make unguarded off-the-cuff comments about colleagues, the business or the parent company (where it applies).
6. When counselling any fellow employee, management or staff, the manager should have total respect for discretion and confidentiality. The course of action to be taken should be agreed with the individual, including which pieces of personal information may be discussed with a specific third party.
7. The human resource manager's behaviour should consistently reinforce the desirable impression of being firm but fair. Human resource management is primarily concerned with a mutually beneficial merger of business and people goals. One should not be seen to be achieved at the expense of the other.
8. Staff should feel that the human resource manager really does have time for them and concern in them. "Open door" policies and "managing by wandering about" are key techniques.

YOUR DEVELOPMENT

The overall relevance of this topic to individuals will depend largely on the specific job they are undertaking, and the career ambitions which they hold for the longer term. General managers, responsible for people issues amongst other priorities, will wish to consider short-term development opportunities designed to improve performance in the current role. Specialist human resource managers who envisage continued progress within the function should consider the necessary career development and training which will assist them to become senior personnel specialists. However, neither party should fail to recognise the significance of effective people management, whatever their ultimate goal. The sensitive judgement and direction of employees is a vital skill to the operational manager and many a Managing Director or Chief Executive will have spent some time in the personnel function.

Management is about getting things done through people and the selection of the right individuals for the management team is a key task for any senior manager. It is also worth noting that many specialist human resource managers are very good at arranging training and development for others but frequently neglect to consider their own learning needs.

On-job development

- The human resource manager should develop an attitude of constantly improving personal performance, re-examining methods, innovating and implementing action.
- He or she should agree personal objectives with the management, and agree any training or development needed to achieve those objectives.
- For every objective, success levels and criteria should be set and agreed, providing important measurement levels against which to judge personal performance.
- From the overall objectives, a monthly activity plan of key tasks to be tackled by certain dates should be developed. (See pro forma in Appendix 2).
- The human resource manager should ensure that his or her superior carries out a performance appraisal with him or her based on the agreed objectives and achievement of activity plans. There should be at least one formal appraisal per year.
- From the appraisal, the further training and development required should be agreed
  (a) to improve performance in the current job and
  (b) to prepare for the next career move.
- The appraisal may also be the ideal opportunity to discuss the career path plan, and begin to direct personal development to longer-term goals and ambitions.
- When established within a supportive and mature team, the manager should review personal progress with colleagues, perhaps asking them occasionally to sit in on interviews and training courses so that they can give honest and constructive feedback.
- Appropriate reference material should be on hand. It is also important to read trade press and journals when possible to keep in touch with employment developments.

Off-job development

- Once off-job training is deemed necessary it is important to investigate various training procedures, specifically assessing whether the programmes meet personal needs and whether they are value for money.

- In multi-unit companies, personal needs should be discussed with the central training manager or company training centre to determine if such development is available within the organisation.
- If it is necessary to seek external training provision, the following organisations should be considered; they should have local offices (see the telephone directory):
  — Hotel, Catering and Institutional Management Association (HCIMA)
  — Hotel and Catering Training Company (HCTC)
  — Institute of Personnel Management (IPM)
  — Training and Enterprise Councils (TEC)
    (Scotland: Local Enterprise Councils (LEC))
  — local colleges, polytechnics and universities
  — training consultancies.
- Remember that off-job development does not only cover training courses, but may be provided through conferences, seminars, association branch meetings (eg HCIMA) and joint venture activities (eg with other local businesses). Considerable numbers of open or distance learning packages are now available.
- Development can also be provided by liaison and cooperation with other human resource managers in the locality and/or within the company. Many towns have active forums and joint committees on employment and training including the local authority, schools and colleges, such as Education and Business Compacts. Human resource managers should become involved and get on to some influential committees, such as an industrial liaison role with a local college.

Professional development

- The importance of membership of the relevant professional management association is increasing rapidly today. It is a measure of ability, experience and absolute commitment to the profession.
- The general manager will no doubt consider the HCIMA as the relevant body. Dependent on previous experience and qualifications, the association membership qualification may be gained through its certificate and professional diploma courses,

provided by many colleges throughout the country. (For further details, see Part 4.)

● For students or corporate members of the HCIMA, personal development opportunities are possible as an active member in the local branch. The branch committee should be contacted.

● The more specialist human resource individual who sees a long-term career in the function should consider membership of the Institute of Personnel Management (IPM). This national organisation is eminent in the wider business community and membership carries a premium in terms of potential career development.

● The IPM has a variety of entry points: management entry may be through a college course, Certificate in Personnel Practices (one year day-release), or through correspondence course or open learning. 170 centres throughout the country offer IPM courses. The central office address and telephone number may be found in Appendix 3. Contact can also be made through branch committee meetings or a local college providing IPM courses.

Educational development

● A number of recent initiatives should be borne in mind when considering personal development in its widest sense.

● There is now a GCSE in travel and tourism, which introduces 14-year-olds to the leisure, catering and tourist industries and provides short work experience opportunities. Leading companies in the hospitality and travel industry are involved. It is possible to be involved locally.

● Previous qualifications and experience may now be worth something. The Council for National Academic Awards has introduced a scheme whereby prior learning and experience may be awarded credits towards higher qualifications. Both the HCIMA and the IPM are involved in this scheme, which is known as CATS (Credit Accumulation and Transfer Scheme). Advice may be obtained by contacting the nearest centre of higher education (eg a polytechnic or business school).

● Also available under the CATS scheme is the accreditation of in-company courses. So, courses run at the outlet or within the corporate training centre may be credit-worthy, providing delegates with more "points" towards a higher qualification.

- Details of all these developments are available through the Hospitality Management Learning Conservation (HMLC) comprising the hospitality departments of four polytechnics: Brighton, Oxford, Manchester, and Napier in Edinburgh. Addresses and telephone numbers are listed in Appendix 3.
- Much of the training and education within the hotel and catering industry is being assessed by organisations such as the HCIMA and HCTC for compatibility with the awards of National Vocational Qualification (NVQ). NVQs will increasingly become a guide to the work-based competences attained by employees, from operatives to supervisors and, ultimately, management.

YOUR TEAM ROLE

Whether a human resource manager is a full-time appointed personnel manager or an assistant manager whose responsibilities include the overseeing of human resource issues, it is necessary to examine how this role fits in to the wider management team. Managers must be clear about the way in which their activities relate to higher management and the rest of the line managers and specialists who make up the "executive team". In this way they will give appropriate attention and commitment to all people issues. Their aim must be to ensure that *they*, and *their personnel and training activities*, are valued by the team as a major contributor to the achievement of business goals.

A human resource manager must be seen as the provider of a functional service to line managers and all employees, *not* as a go-between at the beck and call of demanding operators and temperamental supervisors. There must be general management commitment to the principle of good people management, agreement about the role objectives and authority of the human resource manager, always in line with the business plan and the management's own personal objectives in this area. This will often mean that the human resource manager will need to stand up and influence many a hardened human resource cynic!

The human resource manager should consider the following factors when clarifying his or her role in the management team.

1. The role includes responsibility for recruitment, training and welfare, but to what degree is he or she a coordinator rather than a doer?

Line management and heads of department must carry out their responsibilities, eg for departmental training and staff management.

2. It is necessary to sell the benefits of good human resource management constantly to all members of the management team. Real commitment must be elicited from colleagues by behaviour which displays enthusiasm, demands involvement and shows great persistence.

3. The human resource management role involves the manager in all areas of the business, bringing him or her into regular contact with all types of people, from the shop floor to senior management. This is a unique position from which to assess morale and current or potential problems. This should be used to provide constructive feedback to colleagues and management.

4. It is necessary to be involved when and where it matters (at decision making forums, at business planning sessions, at business update and forecast meetings), contributing and assisting, rather than simply reacting to directives from elsewhere.

5. It is important to be aware of legal positions and statutory obligations as well as current codes of practice in matters pertaining to employment and training, and to ensure that colleagues and higher management are also aware of these responsibilities.

6. The human resource management role must be proactive, anticipating and clearly communicating trends in employment, general concerns and the people implications of operational plans and decisions.

7. It is necessary to be quick in reacting and responding to operational priorities; the human resource manager must be ready to give clear, firm advice to colleagues on procedures, policies, legal factors and just plain reasonableness in employment and personnel matters.

8. The role will occasionally be that of an advisor or arbitrator negotiating between different people and groups within the business. The manager must put the business first but be prepared to stand up for what is right and fair, not just act as a fence-sitting umpire.

9. The manager must coordinate and, within delegated authority levels, control the human resource activity. This will often

include such items as wages, overtime payments, casual payments and holiday requests, but also the upholding of good practice (for example, avoiding recruitment without proper planning, analysis or authority, or taking serious disciplinary action without due regard for procedure or consultation).

10. The human resource management role should encompass the monitoring of communications within the business, from top to bottom in the organisational structure.

11. The manager should be constantly assessing situations and be amenable to innovation and change. The search for improvement and development must never be far from his or her thoughts.

12. It is often necessary to fill the role of informal counsellor within the management team. This may place the manager in some difficult interpersonal and behavioural situations, and for issues involved here, such as confidentiality, consult "Your Behaviour" (page 21).

Part 2
THE
EMPLOYMENT PROCESS

BEHAVIOURAL TRAINING

Training is often referred to as the structured development of knowledge, skills and attitudes. Knowledge may be gained by reading, listening and experiencing. When considering training for new skills and different, but appropriate, attitudes, we are in a situation of changing the ways in which an individual, the trainee, behaves. Employees come with a range of experiences, a set of attitudes built from birth and varying levels of knowledge. Training is adapting that mixed bag of attributes into a systematic, job-oriented set of qualities demanded by the standards and methods of the particular organisation.

For example, a young person may be employed or need to be trained as a sommelier or wine waiter. In the writer's experience people have been given a corkscrew, a book on wine and told to get on with the job. Knowledge was possible, but as far as opening a bottle of wine and interacting with the customer was concerned, there was a distinct lack of assistance.

Knowledge in isolation is of partial use only to the hospitality industry. The business demands technical and social skills. The business *is* customers, with whom staff are in constant contact, so training must reflect this consistently and significantly. The following points illustrate how to ensure that training in an establishment has a strong emphasis on interaction and behaviour.

- All training sessions, on-job or off-job, must link the technical skill of the task to the social skill involved. For example, an hotel receptionist must not be trained in the use of the front desk computer without awareness of the fact that a customer wishing to check in is right there in front of the receptionist.

31

A restaurant cashier must be trained thoroughly on how to use the till, but also to be aware that customers are all around, and may even ask him or her for a table for two.

- All training plans, sessions and manuals should be quality-controlled to include behavioural issues. An operating systems manual is not sufficient.
- "Back-of-house" staff should also receive social skill and behavioural training. For instance, the room maid is often the first person a guest meets; a kitchen steward has a "customer" called a chef.
- The importance of customer care attitudes and behaviour should be emphasised from the start of an individual's employment: induction should not just be about how wonderful the organisation is.
- Role-plays and realistic simulations should be used wherever possible in training. Role-plays can be very effective if linked to earlier knowledge and demonstration sessions, and if the role-play is well prepared and constructive feedback given. (An example is illustrated later in this topic.)
- Training sessions such as role-plays are appropriate opportunities for using video cameras and recorders. This facility must be used carefully and sensitively but it can be extremely powerful in encouraging people to consider their own behaviour.
- Wherever possible, often dependent on the size of the establishment, people should be trained in pairs or groups. Their own interaction and discussion will assist consideration of behavioural issues, and it is cost effective.
- Behaviour is also involved in correcting people. Supervisors should always be aware of the faults and shortcomings of their staff, but not only in technical matters, such as wrongly clearing plates from the left, but social skills such as lack of eye contact and a smile when approaching the table.
- Special rewards and recognition for particularly good behavioural skills displayed by staff should be considered.

Example

If training restaurant staff in wine service, link the technical and social skills in the following manner.

- If possible, get three members of staff together for a 30-minute off-job training period, the first of two sessions.
- Each has a wine list and the restaurant manager takes them slowly through the list discussing the types of wine, characteristics, popularity and price. The importance of wine selection to the customer is stressed. The importance of wine sales to the business is stressed.
- A technical training session on opening a bottle of wine using the "waiter's friend" corkscrew, conducted by the Restaurant Manager, who is HCTC qualified.
- The demonstration is followed by each trainee under supervision, gaining experience by opening bottles of house wine (recorked for use that evening).
- Knowledge should be imparted during the session and by a hand-out to take away, about the service of wine, the major wine-producing regions of the world, and the temperature and method under which wine should be served. (End of first session.)
- The second session begins with a demonstration training session on how to present a wine list, take an order, and serve different types of wine. Reference is made to ice buckets, wine coasters, decanting and other methods of presentation.
- A role-play is set up via a pre-prepared briefing, so that two employees act as customers, and the third employee role-plays the entire process from presentation of the wine list to pouring the wine at the table.
- The role-play should be as realistic as possible – in the restaurant with the table fully laid and all the participants seriously briefed as to their role, whether wine waiter or customer.
- Constructive and helpful feedback is given to each individual, *including* the role-play customers, pointing out all technical *and* social skills involved. Any mistakes (and there will be some) should be treated as important, but the session should be *fun*. People will remember fun more than misery.
- The session ends with hints on tasting wine, and each participant should be given the opportunity to taste and sample the product they are going to serve and *sell*. (End of second session.)

BENEFITS

The provision of high quality benefits to staff is a major contribution towards the recruitment and retention of employees. It also contributes to the morale and well-being of the team.

Good terms and conditions influence an individual to take a job and ensure that he or she is happy to remain in the post for a period of time.

Benefits must be seen as additional to this level of satisfaction and commitment, giving positive motivation to stay and do a good job, and have a better quality of life, inside *and* outside work.

The hospitality industry can offer some obvious and intrinsic benefits due to the very nature of the business. Meals, normally free whilst on duty, live-in accommodation in the hotel business, and the provision of laundered uniforms can be considerable attractions to potential employees. Indeed they should be stressed and promoted much more than they are, with the proviso that the quality of such benefits is vital. "Dickensian" accommodation is not a benefit to anyone; meals of left-overs and chips are hardly likely to motivate; unlaundered and tatty uniforms of the wrong size will do nothing to encourage spirit and pride.

Compared with other industries, hospitality can often be lacking in a range of innovative benefits which show real care and interest in employees. So the benefits an organisation is providing should be reviewed regularly. They need not cost large sums of money. For example, the negotiation of local discounts in shops, leisure clubs and places of entertainment can be done easily through personal contact and trade associations. Some form of reciprocal arrangement may be necessary but encouraging the employees of other businesses to use the restaurant or other facilities at a modest discount is a sensible promotion idea.

There follows a listing of benefits, some established in the industry, others available now from competitors such as retail, building societies and local government services. Consider carefully whether it is possible to extend the existing range of staff facilities and benefits. More detail on major topics (eg staff accommodation) can be found in Part 3 under "Staff Care".

Employee benefits

- Accommodation
- meals on duty

- free non-alcoholic drink on duty
- tea and coffee breaks in recreation lounge
- uniform provided
- free laundry of work clothes
- in-company discounts (eg meals, accommodation)
- taxis for early and late shift staff – free or subsidised
- holidays – four weeks paid per annum
- pension fund: contributory or non-contributory scheme
- social events and trips
- sports events and trips
- sports and recreation association
- local discounts — hairdressers
  - shoe shops
  - clothes shops
  - leisure centres
  - travel agents
  - health and beauty centres
- relocation expenses
- season ticket loan (interest free)
- share option scheme
- building society mortgage and saving scheme
- reduced insurance premiums facility
- compassionate leave system
- medical schemes (eg subsidised BUPA, PPP)
- access to company doctor
- health monitoring — optician (free eye tests)
  - chiropodist
  - breast examinations
  - cervical smear tests
  - blood pressure checks
  - cholesterol testing
  - life-style monitoring (see Part 3)
    (eg smoking, drinking, diet, exercise)
- work place nursery
- access to other childcare facility (address of Working Mothers' Association in Appendix 3)
- hairdresser visitor/discounts
- beautician visitor/discounts for make-up advice
- career break scheme for mothers

- training/learning scheme for personal development (eg Marriott Hotels in United States of America pay for longer-service staff to attend night school courses, not necessarily job-related)
- paternity leave – time off for father at time of childbirth (compare to "Maternity Leave" later in Part 2)
- language training assistance
- performance-related pay/bonus scheme
- internal job transfer scheme (in large multi-unit organisations).

CAREER DEVELOPMENT

Every member of staff should have the opportunity to develop their abilities and, eventually, their career and job prospects. Most people are greatly motivated by the possibility of improving their prospects and potential. Many staff will seek extra responsibility, recognition of success through promotion, and the real increase in status and reward that comes with progression. For the employer this should also be positive and helpful, as people who truly believe that hard work and achievement will be recognised in tangible ways like promotion and job prospects are motivated to stay with their employer for much longer.

However, it is very important for those managing people to realise that not all employees fall into the categories noted above. It must not be assumed that everyone seeks development, nor should an environment be created in which individuals, intrinsically happy to remain in a certain position, feel obliged to strive for goals to which they are not fully committed. Each individual must be treated as such, and efforts should be made to discover their motivations and longer-term ambitions. These will range from the vigorously ambitious individual determined to reach the top, to the highly competent person who values stability and security more than managerial status and responsibility.

Opportunities for in-company advancement clearly vary according to the size and nature of the organisation. Multi-unit companies may have sophisticated internal transfer and training schemes. Such a system should be fully promoted to employees as a valuable benefit so that their career prospects can develop within one firm, assuring continuity of service and associated employment rights.

For single unit operations, the crucial element is the realisation that for an employee to develop it may be necessary for that person to leave the organisation for a job more in keeping with his or her abilities and ambitions. This is hard on the good owner or employer who has trained and developed the individual over a long period of time. However, if internal promotion and development is not possible, it is no use ignoring the situation in the vain hope that the person will stay and "revise" his or her career plans. This always ends in disaster: the person will eventually become frustrated, demotivated and a less than productive worker, and the employment may end in an unplanned and acrimonious fashion.

Consideration should be given to the following issues when reviewing the business' approach to career development of its employees.

1. Discover an individual's personal motivations, ambitions and general life goals.
2. Discuss career development opportunities with an individual at the following stages in the employment process:
   (a) interview
   (b) induction
   (c) on-job training
   (d) with head of department or manager
   (e) at assessments of performance
   (f) at management or supervisory appraisals.
3. Review development for *all* staff. Do not leave out the kitchen porter, the waiter or the hall porter, on the assumption that they will always want to do that particular job.
4. Do not force development on those individuals who are perfectly content to remain as kitchen porters, waiters and hall porters.
5. For people who are likely to remain in a specific job for a long time, develop them within that job by extending and enriching their job-related skills and knowledge. For example, a kitchen porter could be developed in the knowledge of cleaning materials and their proper use and control, both from the cost and "dangerous substances" angle. The kitchen porter could be involved in discussions on these issues with management, the head chef and even the supplier.
6. If career development is sought by an employee, discuss and agree with the individual and his or her supervisor a written plan which gives the individual a measure of confidence that his or her future is being seriously considered by the employer. This plan could cover:

(a) overall career objectives
(b) possible career paths
(c) possible specific career moves
(d) training required at different stages
(e) available in-company training
(f) in-company transfer system
(g) appraisal and progress review points
(h) guide to timing, eg period spent in each job
(i) personal qualities development needs.

7. Careers advice may be obtained from the following sources:
    (a) Hotel and Catering Training Company (HCTC)
    (b) Hotel Catering and Institutional Management Association (HCIMA)
    (c) Job Centre Careers Advisory Service
    (d) local colleges.

CONTINUITY

(See also: ''Succession Planning'')

The principle of continuity in business is fundamental in ensuring that the personnel changes in management, supervision and staff which inevitably occur do not have a negative effect on the success of the enterprise. Because the people who provide the services and products of the hospitality industry are so important, their skills — both social and technical, their personality and character, and their customer knowledge, all become undeniably significant.

Example

A top-class restaurant manager has a pivotal role in not only organising a smooth and efficient food service system, but is the very character of the restaurant. He or she knows some customers by name and remembers their likes and dislikes. He or she can make a good meal become a memorable experience and customers will return to the restaurant, as much for the manager as for the food and ambience. The departure of such a person is a blow in itself but, being practical, this could happen at any time for any number of reasons. If there is then a period of ''relief'' management, possibly not as skilled or charismatic, and without that customer knowledge, then the entire restaurant business is put at risk.

Continuity must be managed and planned. An excellent assistant restaurant manager should be trained and developed as a potential successor: a person who has been spotted as having the necessary talent, and who becomes an understudy, ready and primed for the moment of succession.

From the restaurant manager example, it can be seen how important continuity is to the smaller, personalised business. However, continuity of the business is equally vital to the large catering complex or industrial catering outlet. Only then can the business have some insurance protection and retain its reputation, standards and efficiency. Multi-unit companies, even those with considerable human resources and large human resource departments, still suffer greatly from a lack of foresight and planning. Relief managers are almost a norm, filling in for a few weeks until a permanent replacement is appointed.

The consequences of a lack of continuity

- Vital jobs go unfilled for weeks
- jobs are covered temporarily
- a reduction in standards
- a reduction in profitability (eg through wastage)
- "fire-fighting" becomes the business plan
- training is rushed and incomplete
- promotions are rushed – people are not ready
- unhappy customers strike the firm off their list.

A simple model puts the issue of continuity firmly in the front line of achieving business success.

RECRUIT PEOPLE
↓
TRAIN PEOPLE
↓
PEOPLE ARE ABLE TO DO JOBS/TASKS
↓
TASKS/JOBS ARE NEEDED TO CARRY OUT THE BUSINESS PLAN
↓
BUSINESS OBJECTIVES ARE ACHIEVED

Too many businesses in the hospitality industry fail to plan for and anticipate the future. They are shocked and outraged by the departure of key workers and then complain about the lack of skilled candidates for such jobs.

Human resource management is concerned with being more proactive, less reactive, and more in control of the future. The human resource manager should be constantly reviewing the potential and abilities of all staff and encouraging line management to do the same. He or she should look at the historical labour-turnover figures, consider the known career development plans of key employees, and be a talent-spotter, planning just who, with the necessary training and development, could be developed internally in readiness to succeed.

Further reference should now be made to "Succession Planning", later in Part 2, which gives practical advice on how to go about this crucial step in the employment process.

CUSTOMER CARE

(See also: "Behavioural Training")

Many technically skilled professionals enter the hospitality industry. There are chefs and waiters with City and Guilds qualifications, qualified engineers and accountants, and many more employees who work either in direct contact with the customer, or provide important services which influence the final product or service. All these employees need to be fully aware of customer care. Without constant reinforcement of the reason for being in business — the customer — their jobs are in danger of becoming insular and more important in their perception than the overall objective of the business.

Customer care is a major training and cultural effort in most companies in the service sector. There is no doubt about its contribution to attaining a competitive edge over companies offering a similar product to the market. For example, many hotels in certain star-rating categories offer an almost identical product to the guest. A four-star hotel bedroom, a leisure centre or a coffee-shop restaurant are all offering similar products to their competitors in the same field. The difference is the human element. Customers, particularly in a recession when a buyer's market prevails, will choose to return to the hotel or restaurant that gives them better service and customer care, for this alone gives the customer added value.

Training

The entire training programme of any hospitality enterprise should feature customer care prominently as an issue of the utmost significance to *every* member of staff. Customer care should be part of induction and all on and off-job training. It should be reinforced in notices, staff meetings, management meetings and at every conceivable opportunity.

Supervisors should generally be more vigilant in the observation and correction of social skills, whereas too often they only supervise incorrect technical powess.

Back-of-house staff must realise that they are vital links in the customer care chain and be aware of the motto used in Forte plc recently "If you are not serving a customer, you had better be serving someone who is!"

Customer care is also a frequent cause for refresher training, as the pressure and bustle of constant customer contact can often lead to understandable complacency, even indifference in front line staff.

The role of all management in this area must be to set a high quality example in all their actions and decisions. They should seek out and recognise people who provide an exceptional example of customer care. Too often management is seen as only concerned about profit, reducing costs and reviewing guest services in the light of financial considerations. The management team must share customer complaints so that positive, lasting corrective action may be taken. They must also share the compliments; copies of thank you letters should be posted on to notice boards or communicated at staff briefings and meetings.

DISABLED WORKERS

One often hears the heart-felt cry of line managers for employees who are committed, reliable and who stay in a job for longer than a few weeks or months. Yet disabled workers remain a vast and untapped source of such employees. Given a chance, registered disabled workers or those with special needs will invariably seize it with gratitude, and prove themselves not only capable but outstanding contributors to the business. Too often, however, employers are given to misunderstanding and prejudice, and a lack of behavioural skills when dealing with the disabled. The point is not to be a starry-eyed do-gooder, but to see the employment of the disabled as a sound human resource management issue. They constitute a labour market of potentially excellent workers waiting to be recruited.

The issues

- The term "disabled" covers a wide range of physical problems. Do not immediately think of a wheelchair. Treat every person individually, as employees with "special needs".
- Be aware of a natural prejudice and fear of people who are disabled. Do not just see problems, remind yourself of all the long-term benefits.
- Disabled does not mean unintelligent. There are some brilliant minds waiting for a challenge or an opportunity to focus their intellect. And there are over six million disabled people in the UK alone. Nine per cent of EC citizens have some form of disability.
- When recruiting and interviewing disabled applicants, awareness of behavioural skills will be of considerable benefit to the interviewer and the candidate.

Consider:

- Job adverts to encourage applications from the disabled. The selection process must not "sift out" disabled applicants. At interview, treat the individual no differently to any other. It is important to retain eye contact. Do not be patronising or overly sympathetic and "nice". Discuss the disability frankly and practically.
- Go and seek out applicants from the disabled register by contacting the local Job Centre or Employment Office. Most Job Centres have a Disablement Advisory Service and Disabled Resettlement Officers who can put forward applicants directly.
- The Disablement Advisory Service can also provide details of practical schemes designed to encourage the employment of the disabled. These include:
  - — financial grants for work area design changes
  - — practical equipment and aids
  - — grants for taxi fares to and from work (up to 75 per cent)

- — a job introduction scheme, paying £45 per week for a six-week trial period.
- ● *A Code of Practice on the Employment of Disabled People*, available from the Job Centre or Employment Office gives details on the law and recommendations in this area.
- ● Remember that there are certain legal requirements on employers:
  - — if more than 20 staff are employed, 3 per cent should be registered disabled
  - — if more than 250 staff are employed, there must be a directors' statement in the annual company report detailing the approach of the organisation to the employment of the disabled
  - — lift and car park attendant jobs are designated as *having* to be filled by a registered disabled person
- ● For more detail, obtain the Code of Practice, consult the Job Centre and refer to *Croner's Catering*.
- ● On a training theme, many hotels, restaurants and leisure complexes are now adapting their operations to suit customers with a variety of disabilities. Ensure that staff are trained in awareness of the special needs of these guests, and include such training as an integral part of the customer care training programme.
- ● The Holiday Care Service, a national charity, is able to provide free information and advice on holidays for the disabled and how accessibility may be improved in hotels (address in Appendix 3).

DISCIPLINARY PROCEDURES

(See also: "Staff Handbook", "Termination", "Industrial Tribunals")

Failure to apply disciplinary procedures in a fair and reasonable manner, as outlined in the ACAS Code of Practice, could land an employer at an Industrial Tribunal, with a hefty compensation bill, or some damaging local publicity (or all three). Any firm, small or large, should adopt an approach to discipline which is firm but fair, based on:

(a) *rules* – which are clearly communicated
(b) *procedures* – which are clearly understood

(c) *administration* – which is professional
(d) *reasonableness* – which is displayed in every case.

It is true that employers with fewer than 20 employees do not have to provide written disciplinary rules and procedures. However, when such rules and procedures of overall conduct at work are uncertain and vague, misunderstandings will inevitably occur. Wherever practical, be as detailed as possible. From induction onwards, explain to all employees:

(a) house rules
(b) disciplinary procedure
(c) examples of misconduct
(d) examples of gross misconduct.

Staff must know where they stand, understand what conduct merits a "warning" and what could lead to summary dismissal. This information should be communicated personally via a staff handbook or brochure if financially possible, or by posting the rules on a noticeboard. It should be stressed that disciplinary procedures form part of the employees' terms and conditions of employment, and indeed the procedure can be reiterated within such a written statement of particulars (an example is given later under this topic).

The role of the human resource manager must be to coordinate and orchestrate the procedure, ensuring fairness and correctness. He or she must also ensure accurate and complete administration, all steps in the procedure being documented in detail, all communication between the parties being confirmed in writing, and all written evidence, including witness statements being signed, dated and collated. This documentation can be crucial if a dismissal case ever reaches an industrial tribunal.

Another key role for the human resource manager is to keep line management and supervisors in order. The industry has a history of "instant" decisions, the result of high pressure moments, and these are the very decisions which lead to trouble.

Line management must be clearly informed, as in the example of terms and conditions below, just what level of authority they possess with regard to the disciplinary procedure. No decisions, especially about dismissal, must be taken without full and proper investigation.

The ability to suspend from duty on full pay gives management a valuable breathing space for calm reflection and fact finding.

Written procedures

All these issues may be clearly and unequivocally itemised in a written disciplinary procedure, reproduced in staff handbooks, on notice-boards, or within the terms and conditions of employment. The procedure should consider the following headings:

(a) authority levels of managers and supervisors
(b) disciplinary procedure — verbal warning
           — first written warning
           — final written warning
           — dismissal
(c) examples of gross misconduct
(d) the meaning of summary dismissal
(e) suspension details
(f) appeal procedure
(g) how long warnings stay on a personal file.

For guidance on current practice in the hospitality industry, a full example of written disciplinary procedure is given below. The size and complexity of the business will determine the detail and length of such a statement, but all these aspects are far better dealt with accurately and clearly rather than becoming subject to the inaccuracy of verbal communication.

Example of disciplinary procedures

This procedure applies to all employees from the date of commencement of employment.

Purpose
To provide a basis for the fair and consistent treatment of employees where there is considered to be a breach of company procedures and rules, behaviour constituting misconduct, or failure to meet the required standards of performance in the job.

Authority Levels

Heads of Department/Supervisors have the authority to issue a verbal warning to an employee under their control.

The Line Manager in charge of a specific department has the authority to issue a verbal, written or final written warning. Dismissal may not take place without prior consultation with the General Manager, who alone has the authority to dismiss. Every action must be taken in full liaison with the personnel department.

Disciplinary Procedure Stages

If an employee breaches any company procedure or rule, or fails to meet the required standard of performance or personal conduct, the undernoted procedure will apply:

Stage One – Verbal Warning (sometimes "oral" warning)
The immediate supervisor or manager will see the employee and inform him or her that his or her conduct or performance is below the standard required. Detailed reasons will be given, as well as achievement targets for improvement. This stage should be seen as aiming to encourage and improve the employee's contribution. The warning will be recorded on the personal file. Should there be no improvement after a specified review date, the matter must be referred to the next stage.

Stage Two – First Written Warning
The manager of the department will see the employee and inform him or her that his or her conduct or performance is still below what is necessary. This warning is confirmed, in writing, with further improvement targets, and a review date specified. This meeting should be witnessed, and the notification of disciplinary action (see later) signed by both parties and the witness. The employee may be accompanied by a fellow employee.

Stage Three – Final Written Warning
The manager of the department and the personnel manager will see the employee, who may be accompanied by a fellow employee. The employee will be informed of the action to be taken, the improvement necessary, and that any further failure

to meet the required standard may lead to dismissal. This action will be confirmed in writing to the employee.

Stage Four – Dismissal
In the event of continued failure to meet the standards of performance and conduct required, dismissal will result. The employee will be advised of his or her dismissal, plus the reasons for it, at this meeting. This will also be confirmed in writing, together with an effective date of termination of employment. Clearly, the employee may be accompanied by a fellow employee, and the company represented by the General Manager and manager responsible for personnel.

Gross Misconduct

In the event of an employee committing an act of Gross Misconduct, the procedure at Stage Four will apply immediately. The following list gives examples of Gross Misconduct:

1. Unauthorised possession of Company property, a fellow employee's property or a customer's property.
2. Fraud, or failure to explain satisfactorily accounting, stock, or expenses transactions.
3. Physical or verbal assault, or threatened assault of any person or persons on the premises.
4. Wilful damage of company property.
5. Breach of any health and safety regulation or food hygiene regulation. Breach of other Government legislation, eg Licensing Act, Weights and Measures Act, Fire Precautions Act, Data Protection Act.
6. Smoking in a non-smoking area.
7. Breach of confidential information.
8. Intoxication, by means which renders the employee incapable of performing his or her job effectively, or endangers the safety of the employee or others on the premises.
9. Sexual misconduct or harassment on the premises or on company business.
10. Criminal or civil offences likely to affect an employee's ability to carry out normal duties, or to cause customer dissatisfaction.

11. Negligence, which causes loss, damage, or injury to a fellow employee, customer or supplier.
12. Gambling on the premises.

This list is not exhaustive. The company reserves the right to determine what constitutes Gross Misconduct, based on the facts investigated at the time.

If Gross Misconduct is deemed to have taken place, the employee will be summarily dismissed, employment being terminated without notice or payment in lieu of notice.

Suspension from duty

At any stage of the disciplinary procedure, the employee may be suspended on normal basic pay, pending full investigation into the case. Every effort will be made to investigate the case quickly so that the employee will be seen and given an opportunity to state his or her case no later than five working days after the alleged failure to meet the required standard of conduct or performance.

Appeal Procedure

The employee has the Right of Appeal at any stage of the disciplinary procedure. The reason for an appeal should be put in writing and sent to the Personnel Manager within three working days of receipt of a warning or dismissal.

The Personnel Manager will acknowledge receipt of the appeal request, and will make arrangements for an appeal to be heard within ten working days or as soon as practicable.

The appeal will be heard by the Manager at the level *above* the manager who issued the warning or invoked the dismissal. This manager will be accompanied by a company representative not previously *directly* involved in the particular case.

In all cases, the Appeal may be taken to two levels above the manager who issued the warning or invoked the dismissal and this manager's decision is final. At each stage, the employee will be advised of the outcome in writing not later than five working days after the appeal is heard.

Re-instatement

In the event of re-instatement taking place after dismissal and the subsequent appeal, there will be no loss of continuous service, normal basic pay, accrued holiday, sickness or pension entitlements from the original date of termination.

Accompanied by Fellow Employee

At each stage in the procedure the employee may be accompanied by a fellow employee if so wished. The employee will be given every opportunity to state his or her case fully at the time of the disciplinary or appeal hearings.

Nature of Warnings

In the case of Verbal or Written Warnings, these do *not* have to be for the same offence or similar failure to meet the required standards of conduct or performance.

First and Final Written Warning

In the event that it is considered that the penalty for the offence falls just short of dismissal, it will be deemed as Serious Misconduct, and a First and Final Written Warning will be issued. Any further offence may then result in dismissal.

Review of Warnings

Warnings will remain on personal files for a period of twelve months, following which they will be reviewed by the relevant manager. In general, if there has been a period of satisfactory conduct and performance for six months continuously without a further warning, then they will be removed from the personal file.

First and Final Written Warnings given in respect of Serious Misconduct will never be removed from the personal file.

Disciplinary notification

It is useful to have a standard pro forma on which to summarise all the details of disciplinary action, which can be signed by both parties, and copies taken for both parties. Here is an example:

DISCIPLINARY NOTIFICATION

Name of Employee_____   Date of Incident_____

Position_____   Department_____

Employee informed of right to have fellow employee present_____
(yes/no)

VERBAL/FIRST WRITTEN/FINAL WRITTEN/FIRST AND FINAL WRITTEN

Give details of the reason for the warning, detailing dates and witnesses
as appropriate. Use a separate sheet if necessary:

_____

_____

_____

_____

Employee's Statement:

_____

_____

_____

_____

_____

Action to be taken – standards required: Date to be achieved by:

_____   _____

_____   _____

_____   _____

_____   _____

Employee informed of right to appeal: Yes/No

Employee Signature _____   Date _____

Manager Signature _____   Date _____

In behavioural terms it is important to realise and anticipate the tensions and stresses associated with any stage of a disciplinary procedure. People, on both sides, will become very emotional. After all, reputation, prospects and livelihood are on the line. When "orchestrating" the specific discussions and hearings during a disciplinary procedure, take into account the following points:

1. Be sure that all parties know the time and place of the meeting and confirm the details, if possible, in writing.
2. Be sure that the employee knows well beforehand the exact purpose of the meeting. Tell the employee that "it is a discussion to hear your side . . ." or "it is a disciplinary meeting".
3. Always reiterate the employee's right to be accompanied by a fellow employee, as stated in the disciplinary procedure. Do not allow the meeting to proceed if the employee brings along anyone else (eg solicitor, union representative). Do not allow the inclusion of an inappropriate fellow employee, for example the manager who dismissed the individual.
4. Prepare thoroughly for the meeting, gaining signed statements, collating *all* relevant documentation.
   At the meeting, avoid a confrontational setting, be calm and professional, display firmness and fairness, and consistency.
5. Use eye contact with the employee to encourage him or her to have confidence in you and the procedure.
6. Be prompt in follow-up action, and be detailed in instructions to the employee. For example, in the case of summary dismissal, give the employee all the employment implications of the decision, from outstanding payments if any, to clearance of personal belongings from the premises, to the time and place to collect his or her P45.

Further reading: a free publication from ACAS, *Discipline at Work*, provides practical guidance.

DISCRIMINATION

(See also "Overseas Workers")

The laws and codes of practice regarding discimination form a major portion of the overall struggle for "equal opportunities". In recruitment, selection and the management and treatment of all employees, human resources managers must be aware of the laws which legislate against discrimination. Selection procedures should constantly be reviewed in this light. Is the firm ensuring that the most able or most suitable candidate gets the job? In particular, it is vital to be sure that the firm is not guilty of racial discrimination, sexual discrimination, or of unlawful prejudice against rehabilitated offenders and overseas workers.

Once staff are employed, then it is unlawful to discriminate against them regarding promotion, transfer, training and development or any other staff benefits. It is also necessary to guard against discrimination in disciplinary cases, including dismissal, and in the event of redundancy. There are also increased efforts to ensure equality of opportunity towards other groups of citizens, such as the disabled and the elderly. The latter group is growing rapidly of course and employers will already be raising or abolishing upper age limits in personnel specifications and job advertisements.

All these discrimination and equal opportunity issues arise due to the inbred prejudices of each one of us and of our social or national groups. As an effective human resource practitioner, the important ability is to be able to analyse one's *own* prejudices and bias. To be aware of these traits provides the opportunity to adapt and balance one's own behaviour, influence the behaviour of others, and ensure that the business is run on sound, fair employment principles.

Self-assessment questions

- What are your feelings about black people?
- What are your feelings about Asians?
- How do you view Protestants?
- How do you view Roman Catholics?
- How do you view Jews or Moslems?
- Do you like the English, Irish, Welsh, Scots?
- Would you employ a 55-year-old man as an hotel head housekeeper?
- Or a 40-year-old woman as the restaurant's manager?
- Would you promote a woman who is four months pregnant?

These questions highlight the range of discrimination issues faced by human resource and line managers in their everyday work.

The hospitality industry has the added problem of many set stereotypes and there could be a number of unwittingly discriminatory appointments and promotions as a result. Some hotels want only young females as receptionists, others — such as upmarket London properties — only want men in management positions. Such policies could lead to a tribunal or civil court case: it is not necessary to be employed for two years before instigating a complaint of discrimination (unlike unfair dismissal).

The crucial question to ask, when presiding over selection and promotion, and to test every situation on its merits, is: would the person have been treated any *differently* if he or she had been of another sex or another race?

This "test" can bring out all the pertinent issues and establish that the procedure has been fair.

Apart from the self-examination process to assess personal behavioural patterns and attitudes, there are other actions which should be considered depending on the size and location of the establishment.

1. Check all advertisements for direct and indirect discrimination. Check the wording, job titles and any pictures of employees which become part of the advertising copy.
2. Check that there could be no unintentional discrimination in the advertisement against males, females, married couples or mothers, etc.
3. Monitor the ethnic proportion of the workforce. Does it accurately reflect the local population?
4. Improve the firm's links with any substantial ethnic minorities in the community. Ensure that advertisements appear in any local ethnic press.
5. Remember that there are certain "genuine occupational qualifications" which negate the laws on discrimination, for example, where a specific ethnic catering qualification is required in cases like Chinese or Indian restaurants. Also, an individual with a specific language and cultural background may be needed to handle tourists from a certain country who form a large part of the business of the firm.
6. The rehabilitation of offenders legislation specifies certain periods after the conviction by which the said conviction is "spent". This means that the individual does not have to admit or

reveal the nature of the offence on an application form or at interview.

7. Be alert to potential staff problems, monitoring their language and reactions to people of different nationality and race. This includes the use of "slang" terms such as wop, wog, or dago. (See also "Overseas Workers".)

GRIEVANCE PROCEDURES

There is great value in operating a meaningful, consistent and systematic approach to the handling of employee grievances. Such a procedure should encourage staff sensibly to express their problems to their supervisors. It is better to tackle and attempt to solve a problem quickly, near to its source, rather than allowing people to brood on issues and permit them to evolve into much more serious matters. Such simmering discontent can have appalling effects on everyday relationships and performance.

Grievances should be dealt with quickly, seriously and fairly, and the procedure must be *positively* and *regularly* communicated to staff from induction onwards. Like disciplinary procedures, an outline of the grievance procedure, should appear on the staff noticeboard, in any staff handbook and within written terms and conditions of employment. Such a procedure is a means of really convincing employees that the firm listens, cares and reacts to their problems on an individual or group basis.

The manner in which every grievance is handled is an example which can have great influence on the whole workforce. Too often, immature managers send out the wrong signals to staff regarding the raising of grievances. If staff feel that by instigating the grievance procedure they will be branded as troublemakers, then real improvements and the resolution of underlying discontent will not occur. Staff will lose confidence in the procedure, and in the managers who preside over such a meaningless front. Management will be remote and in the dark as to the real issues affecting productivity, performance and standards.

A high turnover of labour is a natural consequence of the non-listening organisation with a flawed grievance procedure. It really is too late to discover the problem at an exit interview.

Role of the human resource manager in the grievance procedure

- To ensure that all employees understand the procedure
- to encourage matters to be settled at the first stage, namely between employee and supervisor
- to ensure that the written procedure is followed and followed up
- to ensure that line management and supervisors respect the procedure and do not fear it
- to coordinate and administer the procedure, keeping accurate records of grievance procedure meetings and action taken
- to check that action decided upon to resolve the grievance is carried out to the satisfaction of all concerned.

Behavioural issues

Many of the behavioural skills covered in "Counselling" in Part 3 will be most relevant when conducting a grievance interview. All supervisors and managers who may handle a grievance should be properly briefed and trained in how to be most effective.

- Active listening is a key point of behaviour.
- Head nodding encourages the employee to talk.
- Eye contact conveys active interest.
- A calm tone of voice helps.
- Words and statements should be kept simple and clear.
- A neutral non-confrontational setting gets rid of the management/staff divide.
- Do not give instant opinions and solutions.
- Discuss the issue as "our" problem, which "we" want to solve to the mutual benefit of both parties.
- Ask questions to get to the heart of the problem.
- Ask the employee for suggested solutions.
- If there is a work group grievance, ensure that the group elects a representative of their choice.
- Thank the employee for having the "guts" to raise the matter and for using the grievance procedure properly.
- Liaise most carefully with supervisors and managers involved.
- Make clear, full notes of all discussions.

The procedure

Clearly it is desirable for most grievances to be settled at the first level at which they are raised, namely the employee's immediate supervisor or manager. However, some cases need further redress and a procedure such as the one that follows will be determined very greatly by the size of the organisation. In smaller catering operations, for example, the employee may discuss the grievance directly with the actual employer at stage 1 or 2. In multi-national corporations, the case could go up to a company director to give a final decision. A right of appeal should be available at each stage, as in the disciplinary procedure. Ensure that appeals are heard by individuals not previously involved.

Example of a grievance procedure

If you have any grievance for which you are seeking redress, you should apply to your immediate supervisor or Head of Department personally or in writing.

The purpose of the Company's Grievance Procedure is to ensure that if you have a grievance concerning your employment you are able to follow a consistently fair and clearly defined policy.

Stage 1
You should raise the matter orally, or in writing with your Head of Department or Manager

Stage 2
Failing a satisfactory conclusion at Stage 1, you can make a written request for an interview with the Personnel Manager. At this stage a report will be made available by your Head of Department or Manager to the Personnel Manager stating how the matter has been handled to date. At the interview you are entitled to be accompanied by a fellow employee.

Stage 3
Failing satisfactory conclusion at Stage 2, you can make a written request to the Personnel Manager for an interview with the General Manager.

The Personnel Manager will arrange an appointment with the General Manager, or a person appointed for this purpose by the General Manager.

At this stage a report will be made available by your Head of Department or Manager to the General Manager stating how the matter has been handled so far. At the interview you are entitled to be accompanied by a fellow employee.

Stage 4

Failing a satisfactory conclusion at Stage 3, you can make a written request to the General Manager for an interview with a Company Director. The General Manager will arrange this interview, at which stage a report will be made available by your Head of Department or Manager to the Company Director, stating how the matter has been handled so far. At the interview you are entitled to be accompanied by a fellow employee. The decision of the Company Director is final.

It is recommended that no more than three consecutive work days should be allowed to elapse between each stage.

If a matter is raised which affects a number of employees in one department, the grievance procedure will be followed with a representative elected by those employees.

INCENTIVES

(See also: "Productivity", "Wages", "Participation")

Incentives and bonuses are additional measures, over and above an individual's basic terms and conditions of employment, which can be introduced by management in order to increase performance and productivity. These are clearly desirable objectives for the firm, yet incentives also provide tangible, personal rewards for staff who have achieved certain agreed standards and levels of improved performance. Incentives need not be financial in the traditional sense of a wage or salary bonus, but could be gifts, vouchers, holiday breaks or contributory points towards a larger scheme, such as free air-miles. Such schemes help to involve employees in the running and, in particular, the success of the business.

Incentives and bonus schemes must motivate employees to do "that little bit more", for themselves, and therefore the customer and the firm. Such incentives must *not* become seen as an accepted part of the payment package, but should be a relatively short-term measure designed to tackle a specific business issue or problem, eg low sales of spirits in a pub operation. An alternative purpose could be to maximise return on investment, eg an incentive scheme for the opening of a new restaurant.

So, incentive programmes should have a defined "shelf-life". If they go on for too long, for example nine to 12 months, they become just another part of the job and its conditions. This misses totally the real point about incentives: that they are a reward for performance that is over and above the norm.

Hospitality industry schemes

Many schemes in the hospitality business tend to centre on customer contact staff and are a response to sales or profitability crises. Whilst this is quite legitimate, the full benefit of incentives should be spread across departments and can be offered at various times of the year, based on pre-planned topics. In particular, back-of-house and catering services departments should not be forgotten. It is very important to base the entire scheme on a simple, clear objective. For example:

(a) increased average spend in the coffee shop from the current £3.58 to £4.00
(b) labour turnover reduced by 10 per cent
(c) costs of materials reduced by 5 per cent
(d) room checks by housekeeper reveal no faults against a new standards checklist.

Eight steps to a successful incentive scheme

1. Agree the *specific* objective of the scheme (as above).
2. Clearly establish the participants, by *name*.
3. Establish target levels of performance (could be based on productivity norms so that desired achievement is significantly above norm).
4. Ensure targets and time-plan are achievable — staff must believe achievement is possible, otherwise it is a disincentive.

5. Establish a rewards system based on business growth or savings resulting from increased business or productivity. (Refer to company accountant.)
6. Devise a monitoring system which covers the communication of progress for the human resource manager, the business and the participants.
7. Communicate clearly the details of the scheme to all employees involved.
8. At the conclusion of the scheme (the target date), stage an event where all or the leading achievers are presented with the reward, prize or notification of financial bonus. This internal promotional activity can make other employees more motivated to gain "their turn".

Larger organisations should be aware that there are specialist companies which can be contracted to arrange and administer such incentive schemes, including the monitoring of the results and benefits to the business. This evaluation is the acid-test as to whether the scheme has paid dividends to the firm.

Examples of incentive scheme rewards

The rewards planned for successful scheme participants, whether on an individual or departmental basis, should be personally exciting and desirable, not purely job-related (such as extra training provision). Some examples are:

- financial bonus, eg percentage of increased food and beverage sales
- employee of the month award
- employee of the year award
- free air-miles for longer continuous service levels
- shopping vouchers
- meals in other company restaurants
- weekend breaks in other company hotels
- special event tickets (concerts, sporting events)
- sporting trials (ballooning, flying, hang-gliding)
- membership of a leisure club

- free lessons for an activity   —   flying lessons
  - — driving lessons
  - — archery
  - — sailing
  - — diving
  - — language training
  - — aerobics
- catalogue tokens towards items of staff's own choice
- trading stamps
- petrol tokens scheme.

Examples of schemes bases

Some of these examples are easier to administer by the individual and some work better by the department.

Department	Based on:
Restaurant	Average spend
	Wine sales
	Repeat customers
Kitchen	Food gross profit
	Productivity
	Competition success
Bars	Average spend
	Cocktails sold
	Spirits promotion
Front office	Average room rate
	100 per cent occupancy
	Room types sell-up
Housekeeping	Productivity
	Standards check
	Cost of materials
Maintenance	Reduced faults
	Energy savings

Department	Based on:
Kitchen porters	Standards check
	Cost of materials
Reservations	Room sales growth
	Average room rate
Sales team	Conversion of calls to sales
	Sales growth
Personnel (human resource) team	Labour turnover
	Continuity of staffing
Secretaries	Accuracy checks
	Cost of materials
Conference and banqueting	New business level
	Repeat business
	Average spends

From time to time a general issue could be on an across-the-departments basis for an incentive scheme, normally due to a current operational or business plan priority. Examples are:

(a) special promotions
(b) energy conservation
(c) customer complaints
(d) in-house sales
(e) profitability levels
(f) linen and laundry costs
(g) breakage and wastage
(h) guest comment card responses.

It is the job of management to motivate the employees. Incentive and other payment schemes assist in this, but are *not* substitutes. They should be an integral feature of a total management commitment to achieving business goals through the performance of a truly motivated workforce.

INDUCTION

We all know that induction makes sense. We have been tackling it for years, from checklists and brochures to full day events including a video and a quiz. Yet constantly the real effectiveness of planned, professional induction is doubted. It is known that a correlation exists between inadequate induction and a high turnover of short-service employees.

Perhaps induction planners have been asking the wrong question. They have based their induction programmes on their answers to "What do we want new employees to know about us?". The question they should be asking is "What does a new employee want to know?".

Having no induction scheme is a cardinal sin, but too much information crammed into a traumatic first day is equally bad, if well-intentioned. So the next question must be "What do new employees want to know on their *first* day?". The answer to this question is not "where the founder of the firm was born" but where employees are going to work, the people they are going to work with, etc.

Induction should be phased over a period but it is necessary to ensure that new employees get the information they want and need at the right time.

Examine the induction checklist given below and, appropriate to the individual organisation, decide the time-phasing of the information. This could be spread over hours or days, as long as it is appropriate and effective. The "when" column is therefore intentionally blank. A "starter's friend" is a specially selected fellow employee who will help the new recruit settle in and feel welcome.

Induction Programme: plan and checklist

Activity	By whom	Where	When

Greeting on arrival
Personnel
  administration
PAYE and NI
  details completed
Introductions to
  key personnel
Tour of premises
	Personnel Officer
	and
	General Manager
		Training room	

Activity	By whom	Where	When

First Day Essentials
Tour department
Cloakroom and toilets
Lockers
First aid
  arrangements
Fire precautions
Entrance, exit
Employee restaurant
Telephone
Noticeboards
Uniform needs
Live-in
  accommodation
  (if appropriate)
	Supervisor
	"starter's friend"
		In department	

Terms and Conditions
Explained
Particulars explained
  and given
Working procedures/
  breaks
Wages procedures
Holiday arangements
Sickness rules
Benefits, etc.
	Personnel Officer
	and Wages Clerk
		Personnel and
		Wages Office	

Job Purpose
How it fits into
  department
Department's
  function
Outline of operation
Training to follow
Meet colleagues
Outline of standards
The customer – our
  business
Customer care
	Supervisor
	Manager
		Department	

Activity	By whom	Where	When
Training and Development Statutory training outlined Job skills training discussed Possibility of promotion In-company transfers Methods of assessment	Training Officer	Training room	
Health and Safety Personal responsibilities Safety rules Hygiene requirements Future statutory training Fire precautions training Accidents procedures First aid supplies Health issues	Training Officer and Supervisor	Training room	
House Rules Establishment's regulations Examples of misconduct Disciplinary and grievance procedures Appeals procedure Handbook issued	Personnel Officer and handbook	Training room	
Staff Communications Staff meetings Departmental meetings Consultative committee Newsletters Noticeboards Suggestion box	General Manager	Meeting room	

Activity	By whom	Where	When
The Company History Organisation Business plans Company benefits Induction review quiz	Personnel Officer and Training Officer	Training room	

INTERVIEWING

Most decisions on the selection of a particular applicant will be taken following and based upon an interview. Psychometric testing, assessment centres and graphology techniques may be available, but most people who get a job in the hospitality industry in the next ten years will obtain it after an interview. Therefore, it would be sensible to consider how such an interview can be made more "scientific".

Interviewing skills are not just confined to recruitment. Many of the same qualities are required in disciplinary, grievance and counselling meetings. As in so many behavioural situations, preparation is very important, both data-led as in scanning the specification of the job and applicants, application form and any other relevant documentation, and in putting oneself in the position of the candidate (the empathy factor).

To get the best out of the interview it is necessary to consider the following:

1. The likely initial behaviour of the candidate.
2. One's personal behavioural situation – prepared? too busy? under pressure?
3. The interviewer must help the candidate:
    (a) Where will the candidate wait?
    (b) Who will welcome the candidate?
    (c) Have other staff and colleagues, the receptionist or secretary been briefed?
    (d) Who will offer refreshment?
    (e) How long will the candidate be kept waiting?
4. The interviewer should greet the candidate personally, shake hands and give first name and surname. Move to a private office.

5. The office should be tidy and professional in appearance, with the candidate's application or CV in a prominent position. This demonstrates good preparation.
6. Barriers (such as desks) should be kept to the minimum: a better solution might be chairs around a coffee table.
7. Welcome the candidate and repeat personal introduction, with an explanation of job title and position in the firm. Explain the purpose and scope of the meeting (eg it may be the initial interview to be followed by a second one with a line manager or head of department).
8. Ask open questions, maintaining eye contact and using the interviewee's first name frequently. Sit in relaxed (but not horizontal) posture. Ensure that there are no interruptions of any kind.
9. Encourage the candidate to start talking about him or herself, by picking an easy subject early on (eg career to date).
10. Listen actively and intently, using appropriate gestures and eye contact, and taking notes sensitively when appropriate. Maintain a professional interest.
11. The interviewer's tone of voice should be calm and relaxed, yet positive and assertive. Questions should be concise and assertive enough to elicit an appropriate answer to the question asked. Use the "funnel questioning" technique to pin a candidate down to specifics (see below).
12. Keep a discreet eye on the time.

Example of "funnel" technique

Topic: previous job as Restaurant Manager at "Le Corsaire"

Tell me about your position at "Le Corsaire".

What were your responsibilities?

What were your priorities?

Your achievements?

Sales growth?

Average

spend

growth?

- Non-verbal behaviour may be used to reflect increasing assertiveness (eg sitting forward, harsher tone of voice, direct eye contact) as interview progresses.

- Explore each major item: career experience, ambitions, the particular job opportunity, style of working, personal circumstances.

- Supply information by summarising job details and company situation.

- Ask if the candidate has any questions and then conclude with a plan of further action — what happens next; second interview; contact by telephone or post; when.

- Be thorough and professional, even with a poor prospect, because the company's image and that of oneself is at stake.

- End the interview with a firm handshake and direct eye contact; smile and escort the candidate to the next interview or to the exit.

- If the candidate is being passed on to a second interview, make sure that the manager or head of department is prepared and has the time and the relevant documentation. He or she should have been briefed before the interview and it is necessary to confer with him or her as soon as possible afterwards to arrive at an early decision.

- It is useful to complete a written interview assessment. A simple example is given overleaf.

More complex assessments, for supervisory and management positions are based on classification systems such as Munro Fraser's five-fold system:

(a) impact on other people
(b) qualifications and experience
(c) abilities, aptitude for learning
(d) motivation, achievement-oriented
(e) personality adjustment, emotional stability.

Example

Interview Assessment Form

Position:

Applicant:

Interviewer: Date:

Reasons why applicant suitable:

Reasons why applicant unsuitable:

Job offer: yes/no

Details of offer:

Date of starting:

Accommodation: yes/no

LABOUR MARKET

Detailed knowledge and analysis of the firm's supply of labour is a vital factor when formulating human resource strategies towards recruitment and selection. Knowing the market means answering the following questions:

(a) Where does labour come from?
(b) Who is the firm's labour?
(c) What do they want from work?

The business may consider a variety of sources of labour depending on the type and scale of the organisation:

(a) local
(b) national
(c) overseas.

By analysing workforce needs, and composing a set of strategic and tactical measures to get the required people, it is possible to plan an effective annual recruitment programme. This process must involve a thorough analysis of the labour market; for most hospitality businesses this means the local potential supply of workers.

The characteristics of that potential supply determines how it is to be tapped, the training which new employees will need, and how they will need to be managed and developed.

For example, areas where manufacturing industry has declined sharply in the 1980s are now providing many potential workers for service industries, but clearly they have special needs for training and readjustment to a totally new industry and job philosophy. Indeed, the hospitality business is attracting more and more labour with no previous experience in the industry; a recent survey showed that the proportion was 50 per cent.

Labour market characteristics

The following are some of the characteristics in the labour market.

1. Local population profile:
   (a) age profile

(b) types of housing estates
(c) social economic grouping
(d) local employment levels
(e) local industry state.
2. Ethnic minorities:
(a) service culture
(b) tradition.
3. Religious concentrations:
job taboos
4. Female potential:
(a) working mothers
(b) women returners
(c) part-time needs
(d) casual work needs.
5. Workers from other industries:
(a) recent redundancies
(b) overseas workers
(c) seasonal tourist centres.

The importance of this type of information is that recruitment and other human resource activities must be organised to fit in with the profile of the labour market.

It may be necessary to reorganise jobs and rotas, and review terms and conditions of employment, such as the provision of live-in accommodation if recruiting significantly beyond the local area.

Today's labour market requires increased flexibility of approach, and instead of the old attitude of setting the hours and shifts and expecting the labour market to "tow the line or else", it may be necessary to start asking the labour market, "What hours can you work?".

Labour market networking

A good human resource manager learns to nurture his or her labour supply. It is necessary to keep in touch, get involved and become known in the market and in the community. Networking the various parties and elements of the market should be a planned, systematic strategy, rather than a case of "perhaps I may bump into so-and-so at the HCIMA branch meeting". Here are some thoughts on how to be an effective networker:

(a) send mail-shots to local housing estates

(b) communicate new business developments

(c) use the free local press for articles, PR, job advertisements and news of human resource improvements, like a new staff restaurant or shift system

(d) put regular advertisements in the national trade press, eg *The Lady* or *Caterer and Hotelkeeper*, or a newspaper in the area of supply

(e) use the ethnic press where appropriate

(f) visit schools and colleges, both national or overseas if necessary. Get them to visit.

(g) develop a good rapport with the local Job Centre

(h) keep in touch with aquaintances and colleagues in other areas of the country or overseas

(i) be active in HCIMA branch, or IPM, or British Hospitality Association (formerly British Hotels, Restaurants and Caterers Association).

LABOUR TURNOVER

High labour turnover is a long-standing *bête noire* in many sectors of the hospitality industry. It leaves an unhealthy impression on potential recruits and can have dire consequences for an individual business which experiences operational problems, and a reduction in standards and profits. Line management and supervisors need to be constantly reminded of the true (hidden) costs of labour turnover.

Every incidence of turnover and replacement involves time, material and performance costs, from recruitment, to administration, stationery, training, wastage, low productivity and possible loss of business.

Regular customers like to see the same face at least twice. Consistency is fundamental to a successful catering operation and labour turnover can seriously damage continuity.

Conservative estimates suggest that every leaver/replacement exercise costs £700. Reducing labour turnover requires detailed analysis of and reaction to its many causes. The important point is not just to concentrate on recruitment but to give retention the same emphasis.

The human resource manager's role should be to set up an effective, meaningful monitoring system. Overall business turnover can be an accurate indicator in a small firm, but larger organisations should consider turnover on a departmental basis. Any system should be accurate, proactive and relate turnover in terms that business people understand (i.e. costs). It should reveal trends — particular problem jobs or departments — so that line management can be alerted and take the necessary operational decisions.

One of the most frequent problems with labour turnover figures is not just the relevance to a department, but the meaning of the figure, eg:

(a) What is the base level?
(b) How many staff are there in the business or department?
(c) Is there an in-built turnover anyway (eg seasonal staff, students, transient overseas staff, industrial placements from colleges)?

A business may actually *want* a particular level of labour turnover. This can be the case in high-pressure, customer-contact jobs such as that of a counter-hand in a fast food outlet, or high volume cafeteria and coffee shop. It may be asking too much of any individual to maintain a total customer care approach in such a business for more than nine or twelve months. At some time, pressure, difficult customers and repetitive tasks will affect performance. Therefore some turnover may be expected and planned for.

Targets

The most meaningful approach is to establish target labour turnover levels on an annual basis, taking into account the peaks and troughs of trade, and to use these more effectively to measure retention. Such "budgeted" turnover figures need to be agreed clearly with the head of department and can be a component part of the annual recruitment plan. This approach is more analytical and measurable than the broad-brush method of quoting an annual figure, which fails to account for the complex composition of the workforce, the types of outlet and jobs, and factors such as seasonal trading.

As significant as the figures themselves are the reasons for this experience of damaging turnover. Analysis is necessary, and this topic is covered under "Termination". Exit interviews can reveal some useful information, but they are often blandly unhelpful or simply too late.

Lateral thinking may be useful here: ask some longer service staff "Why do you stay?". Once the essentially personal reasons are eliminated, this question can highlight positive and negative factors, which can then be addressed.

Management often does not seem to know why their unit has a particularly *low* level of labour turnover, often attributing it to a "family atmosphere". The question above, applied intelligently, may uncover just what the elements of the "family atmosphere" are; they can then be consolidated.

Recording labour turnover

All businesses need some method of recording basic data. Small firms should at least operate a "starters and leavers" book, and note the reasons for leaving within it. For larger businesses, the starters and leavers book could be departmentalised for easier analysis, and indeed an analysis sheet such as the one suggested below could be used. The very large employers will certainly require a starters and leavers system, and an analysis pro forma; where feasible this can be done through the computerised personnel information system.

Example

DEPARTMENT:		PERIOD:		BUDGETED LTO:	
Length of service	Sex	Voluntary leaver	Dismissed	Redundancy	Total cost @ £700pp
Less than 1 month	M F				
1 to 3 months	M F				
4 to 6 months	M F				
7 to 12 months	M F				
1 to 2 years	M F				
Over 2 years	M F				
Total	M F				

Analysis:

Number employed at start of period:

Number of leavers during that period:

Number of starters during that period:

Number employed at end of period:

Average number employed during period

(ie $\dfrac{\text{total at start of period} + \text{total at end}}{2}$):

Departmental labour turnover:

$$\dfrac{\text{Number of leavers during period}}{\text{Average number employed during period}} \times 100 = \qquad \%$$

Departmental stability index:

$$\dfrac{\text{Number with more than one year's service}}{\text{Total employed one year ago}} \times 100 = \qquad \%$$

MATERNITY PROCEDURES

When an employee becomes pregnant this should be a matter for congratulations. This section looks at how to interpret the maternity regulations and deal with the case of an employee who is pregnant.

As with other legislation it is advisable to have a clear, written statement of policy which should cover the following aspects:

(a) entitlement
(b) length of service criteria
(c) time off for ante-natal care
(d) maternity leave
(e) statutory maternity pay.

This information should be included in any staff handbook or induction pack, and may be included as a section in the written terms and conditions of employment.

The announcement

At the meeting where the employee announces that she is pregnant, the human resource manager must be sensitive, concerned for the individual. He or she must not indicate a miserable foreboding of the potential problems for the organisation that may result from this situation.

It would be sensible to ask "How do you feel about being pregnant?" This question will bring forward a response from which the manager can take a behavioural lead. Do not assume that the employee is delighted. There are many single female workers in the hospitality industry and unplanned and unwanted pregnancies do happen. In such an unfortunate case the employee should be encouraged to seek expert counselling through a GP. In addition it would be sensible at this stage to find out who knows about the pregnancy. There is a strong element of confidentiality to be respected and the extent of that responsibility should be established early on.

Beyond these matters, the first discussion should aim to give a general outline of the somewhat complex arrangements and procedures associated with maternity leave. It should touch on:

(a) entitlements based on actual length of service
(b) time off for ante-natal care
(c) the right to return to work if entitled
(d) statutory maternity pay (SMP).

A summary of entitlements is given below:

Entitlements	Conditions
Ante-natal time off	Irrespective of length of service. Irrespective of hours per week worked.
Right to return to work	Full-time two years' service. Part-time (8–16 hours per week) five years. Service taken to start of 11th week before expected date of confinement. *Note:* small firms of five employees or less, may be exempt from this obligation.
Statutory maternity pay	26 weeks' continuous service ending with 15th week before expected week of confinement (EWC).

Entitlements	Conditions
Statutory maternity pay *continued*	Still pregnant at 11th week before EWC.
	Have stopped working wholly or partly.
	Provided employer with notice of maternity absence.
	Provided employer with form MATBI (maternity certificate).
	Not living outside EC or in legal custody at any time in the first week of maternity pay.

At a further meeting or meetings more information should be given to the employee, on the following lines.

Ante-natal care

The employee should be asked if she has already been to the ante-natal clinic. It should be explained that she is entitled to paid time off to attend. Following her first attendance she must bring in to work her appointment card of future dates and times, and should also obtain a certificate of pregnancy from her doctor or health visitor. The human resource manager must liaise with her supervisor or manager regarding dates and times so that rotas may be planned well in advance.

Right to return to work

If the employee qualifies for maternity leave and the right to return, she must be informed that the law gives her the right to return to work up to 29 weeks after the birth. This 29 week period begins with the week when the baby is born. She must be advised that, as is contained in the policy statement, she can return to her former job, or to a suitable alternative position, as long as the terms and conditions are no less favourable. Small firms of five employees or less can gain exception from this obligation by showing that to uphold it would not be "reasonably practicable" and that a suitable alternative does not exist.

Maternity leave procedure

The employee should be given a copy of the written procedure for maternity leave for her reference. This should highlight first that she must put in writing to the firm the following, at least 21 days before taking maternity leave:

(a) confirmation that she will be absent to have a baby
(b) that she intends to return to work
(c) the expected week or date of confinement, together with
(d) a certificate of the expected week of confinement (EWC) signed by a GP or a midwife.

The human resource manager's obligation, as the person responsible for the firm's personnel function, is to write to the employee no earlier than 49 days from the date of confinement requesting written confirmation that she intends to return to work. The employee must provide the date of return at least 21 days in advance. She may extend the absence by up to four weeks on the basis of a medical certificate. The firm may also extend or delay the return by up to four weeks for a specified operational reason.

It should be pointed out to the employee that on her return the entire period will be treated as continuous service, though holiday entitlement and pay will not have accrued.

Statutory maternity pay

The handbook or particulars of employment could carry an explanation of SMP for the benefit of female employees. For further details see *Croner's Catering*.

During maternity leave

Once the employee has gone on maternity leave, she should not be forgotten. Keep in touch, phone her occasionally if possible, send her newsletters and information about the business. Remember to send a card and flowers after the baby is born and generally maintain the best of relations.

Plan her return well in advance, such as by redeployment of temporary cover or earmarking a suitable alternative position for her.

Keep accurate records of all maternity procedures as the timings and weeks are very significant in determining the woman's rights.

Some additional points

- Dismissal because of pregnancy is unfair automatically unless:
  - the employee's condition makes it impossible for her to do her job adequately
  - she cannot continue to work without contravening the law (eg exposure to harmful substances).
- Some courts have deemed that dismissal due to pregnancy where the woman has insufficient service to claim unfair dismissal could be construed as sexual discrimination.
- SMP liability ends when the employee has received the maximum 18 weeks payment, or works for the employer at any time during the maternity pay period (MPP), or works after confinement for a new employer during the MPP.
- Some seasonal workers could qualify for SMP even if not actually employed during the qualifying week.
- Records should be retained for three years in case of inspection by the Department of Social Security (DSS).
- The DSS has published a useful free guide entitled *Employer's Guide to Statutory Maternity Pay*.
- Some companies are providing maternity benefits above the minimum (eg Shell UK now gives its employees six months' maternity leave on *full* pay).
- If an employee becomes pregnant *again* while *still* away from work, she is entitled to another full period of maternity leave.

OVERSEAS WORKERS

(See also: "Multi-cultural Awareness")

Hospitality is an international business and as such the workforce is a reflection of that fact. The opportunity to learn a language, gain experience in another country, travel and education can be the reasons for people moving to a job in a foreign place.

For the employer there is a simple need to fill vacant positions and to import talent and experience when home-grown skills are in short supply.

Knowledge of how to employ overseas workers, particularly those requiring a work permit, is a key attribute in further ensuring that the firm recruits the best possible candidates.

Such a procedure, if a work permit is required, will take about three months, so it is necessary to plan ahead and sensible to restrict the process to senior skilled jobs.

The application form should require the candidates to state their nationality and, if they are non-EC nationals, passport number and work permit details.

In January 1992 Portuguese and Spanish workers join nationals of the other 10 Member States in not requiring a work permit within the EC.

EC nationals of Member States have the right to the same treatment as British citizens with regard to pay and conditions.

Work permit application procedure

The procedure is as follows:

1. Contact the Department of Employment through the Job Centre – overseas labour section.
2. Form "OW1" may be obtained from the Job Centre.
3. Give details of:
   (a) the job
   (b) job description
   (c) the person
   (d) the purpose
   (e) steps taken to recruit in UK
   (f) CV and references.
4. Check if an entry visa is also required.
5. The permit will take 8-12 weeks to arrive, and will be for a *named* person in a *specific* job, for 12 months.
6. Renewals are possible but can take up to two months to obtain so it is necessary to plan ahead.

There are a number of guidelines about who is likely to be granted a work permit and under what circumstances.

1. The age limits are 23-54 years.
2. There must be no suitable resident labour available.

3. Senior positions must be filled by workers with five years or more in a skilled capacity (hotel and catering school courses can count towards the five years if these were at least two years long).
4. For supervisory levels, the limit is a minimum of two years experience.
5. Permits will be granted to those on training programmes or in a supervisory capacity, especially where they will return to their country with improved skills.

It is sensible to avoid employing large numbers of foreign nationals from the same country. Ethnic "majorities" can be difficult to manage and they may all leave at the same time.

Workers coming from overseas should be fully briefed and the firm thoroughly prepared for their arrival, accommodation and induction.

It is necessary to ensure that colleagues in management and supervision are respectful to all nationalities and races, and training and awareness of multi-cultural issues should be instituted wherever possible.

Permits are not required by British Commonwealth citizens with the right of abode, citizens of Gibraltar, or EC nationals and their families.

If a foreign national has worked in the UK for four years under a renewed permit, that employee may apply for "settled status", when no further permit will be necessary.

Some Commonwealth citizens without right of abode may have no need for a permit if at least one grandparent was born in the United Kingdom.

Doubts about nationality and work permit requirements should be taken up with the Home Office.

Further reading:
(a) leaflets OW5 and OW21 from the Department of Employment (free)
(b) *Croner's Catering.*

PERFORMANCE APPRAISAL

To develop the talents and abilities of employees and to maximise standards of performance should be the objectives of any performance appraisal scheme. Such a scheme should be simple, clear and business-oriented. Yet many such schemes fall into disuse as managers lose interest, doubt the worth of appraisal and, finally, just never find the time to operate them.

The system should be appropriate to the number of employees involved and should be simple, easily understood and straightforward to implement.

Why have an appraisal or assessment scheme?

- To assess employee performance
- to develop employee abilities
- to assess employee potential
- to determine future training
- to assess oneself as a manager.

How does it benefit the business?

- By improvement of standards
- improvement of efficiency/productivity
- improvement of communications between management, supervisors and staff
- helps to plan training
- helps to plan succession
- helps when determining wage reviews
- can be a useful back-up when taking disciplinary action or justifying dismissal at a tribunal (but it can also be a problem here if it is an inaccurate or bland assessment).

Questions about setting up an appraisal scheme

- What are the objectives of the scheme?
- What method of appraisal should be used?
- Who should be appraised? Answer: everyone.
- How often?
- Who will carry out appraisals?
- Who needs to be trained in how to appraise?
- Who ensures follow-up to appraisals?

The appraisal process

A simple format which can be applied to all employees, in varying depth dependant on seniority and responsibility, is as follows:

Step 1   Review job description and responsibilities.
Step 2   Appraise past performance.
Step 3   Set future targets.
Step 4   Plan training, development and career prospects.

Staff appraisal format

The following format can be used for all hospitality staff, as an annual appraisal or as a review of performance after 3-4 months in the job.

Example

Name:	Job:	Date:

Time in post:	Dept:	Appraised by:

Job description review:

Performance Assessment

Ratings	1	2	3	4
	Excellent	Very good	Average	Needs improvement

Attendance

Appearance

Personal qualities

Job knowledge

Volume of work

Quality of work

Safety awareness

Customer care

Teamwork

Appraiser's Summary

_____

Appraisee's Comments

_____

Signatures and Date:

_____

Copies To Personnel Dept. and Head of Dept./Manager

_____

Personnel Use: Date received:

_____

Supervisory appraisal format

A more in-depth approach may be required and some additional criteria may be needed for assessment when conducting the appraisal of a more senior employee. The following suggestion uses a scale to rate effectiveness, and includes elements of supervisory or managerial abilities.

Example

Name:	Job title:	Date:

Time in post:	Dept.:	Appraised by:

Overall Performance

Tick the box below which best summarises the overall performance. Your rating should reflect: success in work objectives, method of achieving objectives, and general approach and commitment.

Rating – 1, 2, 3 or 4   *Description*

1) *Well above standard expected*	Performance and achievements above expectation or standard required.	☐
2) *Attained standard expected*	Performance and achievements satisfactory; most objectives and standards required attained.	☐
3) *Below standard expected*	Performance and achievements falling well short of expected standard. Can improve with development.	
4) *Unacceptable standard*	Performance and achievements consistently below standard. Major improvement plan needed.	

Job Description Review:

Performance Criteria:
Technical knowledge   *Comments:*   *Rating
1, 2, 3 or 4*

*Ability to plan/
organise daily work
load*

*Ability to plan/
organise long term*

*Administrative
capability*

Delegation skills

*Reliability and
commitment*

*Personal social
skills and
communication skills*

*Training and
development of own
staff*

Teamwork

*Creativity and
innovation*

Appraiser's Summary

Appraisee's Comments

Further goals and targets
What are the three or four main goals and targets over the next period of time. Summarise how and when these will be attained.

To be achieved	How	When by	Comments

Development

1. Training required

2. Career prospects

Signatures and date:

Copies to: G.M./P.&T./Head Office Personnel received:

This systematic yet straightforward approach will reap benefits in managing hospitality people more effectively. However, if plans and promises do not come to fruition, the appraisal system will soon be seen as a sham, therefore follow-up and "delivering the promise" are both essential.

The appraisal interview

Good systems and intentions can be sunk without trace by poor appraisal discussions.

1. All individuals carrying out appraisal interviews must receive coaching and training.
2. Line managers and supervisors should avoid approaching appraisals as if they were an Inland Revenue tax return.
3. General interviewing skills, as covered elsewhere in this book, are required, with special emphasis on getting the appraisees to discuss their own performance, strengths and weaknesses. Wherever possible, appraisees must "own up" to their failings and not be openly criticised. People are much happier "correcting" themselves, rather than being "corrected" by someone else.
4. Avoid the following pitfalls:

   (a) *The "halo" effect*
   Because the employee excels in one aspect of the job, the appraiser believes him or her to be exceptional in all job functions.
   (b) *The "muckspreader" effect*
   The opposite of the "halo" effect — digging for more failure in the certainty that there is some, and determined to find it.
   (c) *Mr Average*
   An appraiser who shies at being bold enough to say "excellent" or "totally unacceptable", resulting in bland, unhelpful appraisals.
   (d) *The "fatal error" effect*
   Where an appraiser bases the entire discussion on one major problem, perhaps fresh in the mind, disregarding many successes achieved throughout the year.

PRODUCTIVITY

The precise and analytical approach to productivity, using techniques like work study, has tended to be a feature of manufacturing industry. If a company makes motor cars it needs to know how many are made each hour, and how many are produced per employee per cost of a working hour. Service industry finds it more complex to assess productivity due to the fragmented nature of the work.

People in hospitality firms constantly complain of being "rushed off my feet", or say "I never stopped all day", or that "We did a hundred and four covers tonight!", but how *productive* were the hours spent in frantic rushing about?

How profitable were the restaurant covers once the extra casuals and/or overtime were paid? A well-used method of increasing productivity in the past decade has been by the reduction of full-time headcount. Too often this has led to expensive over-use of casual workers, temporary secretaries, and overtime payments at premium rates, all of which eat into profit and *reduce* productivity.

Productivity must be seen as "making more efficient use of basic working hours" (Phillip Lynch, *Personnel Management*, March 1991).

Assessment of productivity

The basis for overall assessment of workforce productivity is unit labour cost, which applies at the normal basic rate for normal basic hours. In practical management terms it means analysing manning levels against business volume, rearranging working hours and shifts to meet the business volume profile, and having a high degree of flexibility in the workforce. Management who care about productivity should be able to move employees from one department with a slack workload to another with a high workload. The trading crisis in early 1991, heightened by the Gulf War, resulted in many redundancies in hotels and restaurants, particularly in London. Many of those redundancies could probably have been avoided if the workforce had been trained to be multi-skilled and flexible.

What can improve productivity?

- High standards of attendance and time keeping
- uniforms ready, employees dressed and ready before work
- precisely timed breaks
- clear rotas, planned in advance against business forecasts
- efficient training, and cross-department skills training (eg reception/housekeeping, bars/banqueting, accounts/restaurant)
- clean equipment, ready for use and maintained properly
- equipment cleaned "as you go"
- overtime and casual payments strictly controlled and used as the exception rather than the rule
- regular performance reviews, assessments and appraisals, with efficiency and productivity as key factors

- personal problems and inter-staff communication issues dealt with effectively and quickly
- flexible hours arrangements.

Flexible hours

Flexible hours arrangements are occupying the minds of many managers throughout manufacturing and service industries. The basic premise is that staff work when they are most needed and when productivity can be maximised. Many schemes are based on variable hours; sometimes agreements are fixed with employees that they will work extra hours, perhaps ten, on days of high business levels, and perhaps only six or seven on slacker days.

Other schemes, including those in catering outlets, present staff with a "menu" of hours and shifts which can be selected by employees. As evenings, weekends are therefore "volunteered" for, normal rates are deemed to apply and productivity is not damaged by premium overtime payments.

Many service industries, notably retail outlets and the major supermarket chains, have employed part-time staff to fill particular slots in the daily schedule for many years, at basic rates, rather than asking full-timers to do overtime at higher rates.

Annual hours agreements

More radical measures being experimented with could also have interesting applications for productivity and flexibility in hospitality establishments. "Annual hours" schemes are being agreed con- tractually whereby employees are allocated an annual number of working hours. This method gets away from traditional shift and weekly hours and rosters, and staff can be assured annual job security and pay.

Seasonality of the business means that staff will work much longer hours and more days per week at certain times of the year. One example, given by Phillip Lynch, is of a photo-processing company which has a seasonality cycle similar to that of many hotels and restaurants, including high business volume during the holiday and Christmas periods.

Annual hours arrangements cut out the need for less efficient temporary staff, assure staff of more permanent positions, and increase productivity (based on orders processed per man-hour) by up to 20 per cent.

Bases for productivity

For productivity analysis to be meaningful it must be based on a realistic unit labour cost. The above example of "orders processed per man-hour" is effective in the example quoted (processing photographs). However, hospitality workers perform a variety of tasks which are not always so readily linked to a measurable outcome. Nevertheless, below are some examples which could be used as a basis for productivity measurement, and therefore as a platform for launching incentive schemes and performance-related pay:

- number of covers per kitchen man-hour (white hats)
- number of covers per kitchen man-hour (steward, KPs)
- number of covers per restaurant man-hour
- liquor sales per barperson/wine waiter
- banqueting sales per banqueting staff man-hour
- rooms revenue per reception man hour
- rooms revenue per housekeeping man-hour
- rooms serviced per housekeeping man-hour
- rooms serviced per room maid
- number rooms serviced per room maid hour
- confirmed sales revenue per sales staff.

QUALITY ASSURANCE

The provision of a quality product and service to the customer is an essential aim of the successful business. Quality needs to be defined carefully for every product and service and assured to the customer, whatever its nature.

Further, total quality management (TQM) is about the entire method of operation. It embraces customers, suppliers, employees and every procedure and system by which a business is managed. The whole subject of quality assurance has been catalysed by the promotion of and media attention given to British Standard BS5750. This may be awarded to a business which fulfils a wide range of quality management criteria, and at the time of writing a number of hospitality organisations are actively seeking this distinction.

The effective management of people is a fundamental part of ensuring that the defined standards of quality product and service are attained and then maintained. In particular:

(a) management responsibility for quality service standards must be clearly defined
(b) training must be provided to ensure that staff are qualified to deliver the required standards
(c) training should be recorded to provide documentary evidence of achieved competencies
(d) a corrective training system should be used to address flaws in quality provision
(e) there must be total organisational commitment to quality and
(f) dedication to teamwork amongst all levels of employees.

The direct implication for human resource managers is that they must ensure that the people element of the business is in total integration with business objectives on quality. In this way, employees must be seen as the customers of the human resource department. The strategy on quality assurance should encompass:

(a) recruitment of quality personnel
(b) an induction scheme which stresses the role of "quality"
(c) effective training and a quality product in itself
(d) communications of high quality
(e) motivation of employees to deliver quality
(f) targets and incentives geared to quality standards.

Information on the acquisition of BS5750 is available from the British Standards Institute Catering Industry Controller on 0908 220908. Grants may be available in parts of the country from a local Enterprise (DTI) office.
Further reading: *HCIMA Technical Brief No. 20.*

RECRUITMENT

(See also: "Interviewing", "Labour Market", "References", "Selection", "Vacancy")

This section deals with recruitment, once it has been clearly established that a vacancy does exist. In particular we will consider aspects of recruitment advertising, application forms and the administration of recruitment.

Recruitment control

The significance and cost of every incidence of recruitment demands that there is strict control of the activity. Line managers and supervisors will otherwise "do their own thing" regardless of vacancy analysis or business plans and budgets, and they will generally replace like with like. Human resource management must coordinate any piece of recruitment with procedures and controls supported fully by the management. The format below is a quick and simple method of installing a sensible and professional approach.

Example of a staff recruitment request

Position:_____   Date required:_____

Department:_____ Replacement:_____ Perm/Temp:_____ Hours:_____

In budget:_____   New position:_____

Reasons for recruitment:

_____

_____

_____

Job description and person specification to be attached if *new* position.

Recruitment authorisation

Department Head: Date:

Human Resources Manager: Date:

General Manager: Date

_____

The recruitment process

- Vacancy established
- recruitment authorised on request
- job description agreed — job purpose
  - — main tasks
  - — accountabilities
- person specification agreed — skills
  - — qualifications
  - — experience
  - — personality
- terms and conditions agreed
- recruitment sources and methods agreed.

At this stage, the line manager, the human resource manager and the boss must be in complete agreement over the process to be adopted. Otherwise there may be conflict and misunderstandings and a situation develops in which someone can shift the blame for an unsuccessful recruitment elsewhere (ie to the personnel department).

Recruitment sources and methods

- Internal promotions or transfer
- word of mouth
- new recruit introduced by member of staff
- Job Centres
- recruitment agencies
- local careers offices and services
- schools and colleges
- employment training schemes — youth training
  - — employment training
- overseas workers
- advertising (see below).

It is necessary to be flexible and innovative in recruitment, particularly in an area of low unemployment. Alternatives to traditional replacement are part-timers, job-sharers, women returning to work and the disabled.

The method of recruitment adopted should also be costed in relation to the importance of the position and the urgency of the need to replace.

Forward planning of recruitment increases the opportunity to try the free and cheaper methods such as word of mouth and Job Centres, rather than the expensive method of putting the vacancy with an agency.

Advertising

Once internal unit or company transfers and promotions have been tried but have not come up with a replacement, then advertising is a normal course of action. The cost varies from free local press, to low priced local newspapers and journals, to the very costly national journals and newspapers. The media used should be appropriate to the position and the recruitment advertising budget.

An inventive example is that of a leading Scottish country house hotel. The main requirement for its summer season was socially skilled waiters, waitresses and room maids. Qualifications and experience were less important than personality and enthusiasm: training was given prior to the season. Every year all the required staff came from one small advertisement costing about £50 in *"The Lady"*, a journal read by mothers who were keen to find their offspring some useful summer employment.

Advertisement process

- Design copy (see below)
- decide on media
- allocate budget
- agree administration of recruitment
- decide how applicants should respond
- decide who receives responses and by when
- decide who "sifts" application forms
- arrange dates for interviews with those managers or supervisors involved
- agree with those involved the process and method of selection.

Behavioural difficulties can arise when personnel managers do not liaise frequently and effectively enough with the line person needing the new recruit. The interested party should be kept informed of personnel actions and progress, and should be reassured that the urgency of the situation is understood.

Particular attention should be paid to the interview day when the line manager or supervisor is required to conduct the second interview. The time and date should be arranged for his or her convenience and he or she should be reminded right up to the actual day. Recruits have been lost because the second interview did not take place on the same day because the interviewer was "too busy" or claimed "no knowledge of the interview whatsoever". By the time a second interview is arranged another employer will have snapped up the good applicant.

Advertising design

Consider the following factors and where necessary gain detailed design advice from the newspaper, journal, or (for large organisations) an advertising agency.

- Look at the press and catering journals and competitors' advertisements for comparison of style and ideas.
- Decide on the most eye-catching style that would suit the business.
- Get cost estimates, usually per column inch, from the publication.
- Consider the seniority of the position.
- Establish the image the employer wishes to portray through the quality of the advertisement.
- Decide the message to get across.
- What are the essential details to include? For example:
    - job title and department
    - parent company identity
    - size and style of establishment
    - wages
    - hours/shift system
    - bonus possibility
    - benefits
    - training and development
    - company promotion possibilities
    - transport or location advantages
    - uniform, meals on duty
    - accommodation
    - qualifications required
    - experience sought
    - personality preferences
    - basic job purposes.

A good advertisement can "pre-select" many potential applicants by the inclusion of specific requirements. Advertisers should also consider:

(a) a logo or designated print style
(b) text style
(c) the use of headings and emphasis on certain words
(d) full information on how to respond to the advertisement.

Application forms

The application form should be suitable to the size of firm and the jobs most likely to be recruited for. A pro forma example is contained in Appendix 2. The principle headings should cover:

(a) personal details
(b) education
(c) qualifications
(d) training courses attended
(e) present job details
(f) previous job(s) history
(g) references (3)
(h) a health questionnaire (see Appendix 2)
(i) details of age, disability, and ethnic origin for equal opportunities monitoring.

Recruitment administration

Coordination of the recruitment process should be systematic and efficient. The firm's image as an employer is at risk if correspondence is not accurate and prompt; if records are not kept; if some applicants receive no acknowledgement or response at all.

- Record all enquiries and application forms issued.
- Record by name all applications received.
- If there is a delay in responding to applications, acknowledge receipt in writing.
- Collate all applications after the closing date.
- Either "sift" applications personally or jointly with the recruiting *line* manager.

- Classify applications into categories and record actions in case of an allegation of discrimination:
  - *regrets*: be sure of your *specific* reasons, though not given to the applicant
  - *possibles*: perhaps suitable for alternative job vacancy
  - *definites*: to be called for first interview
  - *hold on file*: could be at this stage or after first interview if applicant could be suitable for another vacancy in the future.
- Ensure personalised, accurate letters are sent as quickly as possible informing applicants of the outcome of the application or interview.
- Review total responses to the advertisement and its cost effectiveness (whether post filled).
- Review the media and method of recruitment.

REFERENCES

Once a decision has been made to offer a successful applicant a position it will be necessary to take up references quickly and effectively. Whether giving or obtaining references, great care must be taken. Information, by common law, must be accurate and in no way defamatory.

Some employers are quite malicious against a former employee and others will happily provide falsely glowing tributes. In both cases treat each reference with care and compare with others and a personal assessment of the individual. In the former case, bitter personal conflict can lead an innocent party to be dubbed as the guilty party.

When obtaining references it is necessary:

(a) to have the consent of the applicant
(b) to take up three references if possible
(c) for speed, to take a telephone reference immediately (see checklist and record form below). This is mainly to check factual information given by the applicant
(d) to send out reference request letters to referees (example below) for senior positions and to follow-up verbal references.

97

Example of a verbal reference checklist and record

Name of applicant: Position to be offered:

Referees	No 1	No 2	No 3
Referee			
Position			
Company			
Job title			
Service period			
Salary			
Attendance			
Reliability			
Timekeeping			
Health			
Honesty			
Industriousness			
Reason for leaving			
Would you re-employ?			

Reference taken by:

Date:

Other information:

Written reference request

A standard letter and reference questionnaire should be drawn up and receipt of such references should be recorded, perhaps in the starters and leavers book, or on the computerised personnel information system.

Example of reference request covering letter

PRIVATE AND CONFIDENTIAL

To:

Dear . . . . .

Re: . . . . (Maiden Name) . . . .

The above named person has applied to us for a position as _____, and has given your name as a former employer stating that they were employed by you from _____ to_____ as _____.
In assessing the suitability of this applicant, we would be grateful if you would complete and return the form as soon as possible. This information will be treated in strict confidence. Thank you for your help.

Yours faithfully,

Steven Goss-Turner
Assistant Manager

Reference request format

The questionnaire can be a separate document or, more cost effectively, may be pre-printed on the reverse of the covering letter given above. Some employers send a stamped, addressed envelope to encourage a response.

Example of a reference request

Date started: Date terminated:

Job title:

Would you re-employ? Yes/No   If not why not?

Reason for leaving:

Comment on the following

Was the applicant to the standard required for —

    attendance:

    timekeeping:

    performance:

    industriousness:

    sobriety:

    honesty:

Comment on the applicant's health record:

Any other information:

Signed:

Position: Date:

Giving references

- Be accurate, fair.
- When giving a reference for someone you dismissed, ensure no conflict between reference and reasons for dismissal.
- Bearer references should only be given to former employees going abroad to work. Otherwise references should be given on specific request from a prospective employer. It is then possible to give an accurate assessment of the candidates for each particular job.
- Overseas workers, especially on the Continent, treat bearer references, testimonials and the like much more seriously than people in the United Kingdom. They will ask for a Certificate of Employment, a basic record of their employment which is factual rather than an assessment.
- Under the Rehabilitation of Offenders Act it is an offence to refer to a "spent" conviction in a job reference. This would be a case of defamation of character.
- Defamation of character may be alleged in a case of any reference that is malicious in its content, or false and inaccurate.

SELECTION

(See also: "Interviewing", "Recruitment")

The ultimate act of the recruitment process, from vacancy, through advertising to interviewing, is the selection of the most suitable candidate and the subsequent offer of the job. A systematic approach demands that the applicant chosen should most nearly fit the original specification: the person with the qualifications, experience, skills and personal qualities needed to fulfil the job description. The criteria for this assessment will be the individual's employment record, training and qualifications, references submitted by previous employers; and basic aspects such as personal aims, circumstances and "performance" at the interview.

The hospitality industry is one involving constant interaction with other people, based upon specific practical and behavioural skills. Despite this obvious fact, most hospitality employees are employed by employers who have not seen them *do* anything outside of the false situation of a selection interview.

The assessment of the suitability of any hospitality applicant must be based on a selection procedure that exposes as much as possible, not only the knowledge of the individual, but the ability to put that knowledge into practice in a customer and service-oriented situation.

Selection processes

The application form

Following an advertisement that should in itself pre-select a number of applicants the information gleaned from the completed application form should further "sift" out those applicants with unsuitable experience and qualifications. The manner in which an application form is completed will also influence the employer's approach to a certain application.

The interview

Normal practice is for the first interview to be with personnel, and for the second and final interview to be with the recruiting line manager or supervisor. This may be sufficient, but greater commitment could be gained by more, however short, discussions, perhaps with departmental managers or the general manager. In medium to small units this should be possible.

A radical addition to the process could be an interview by the work group. A number of organisations now ensure that potential recruits meet the people they will work alongside, and the opinions of that peer group are taken into account.

The behavioural interview

A standard staff interview is a fact-finding mission and important as such. But by placing applicants in actual situations that they have experienced it is possible to learn much more about their perceptions and behaviour. The following are examples of behavioural interview questions:

(a) How do you feel if six customers are queued up waiting to check in at reception?
(b) How do you react when your Head Chef orders more dinners after normal "last orders"?

(c) When did you last lose your temper at work?
(d) How did you feel on the first day of your staff trainer course?
(e) What was your reaction when a customer complained about his meal?
(f) How would you describe the work relationship in your last job?

The practical assessment

The interview process should undoubtedly include some form of assessment of the practical abilities of the individual.
Examples:

(a) get a cashier to take payment and give change
(b) ask a waiter/ress to clear a table for four
(c) get a chef to garnish a buffet item
(d) ask a barperson to pull a pint or make a St Clements
(e) watch a room maid make a bed
(f) use role-plays to assess social skills
(g) get a secretary to type a letter or take shorthand dictation
(h) ask candidates to add up a drinks or accommodation bill.

Additional selection criteria

The depth and length of any selection process must be appropriate to the vacant position. The methods described so far, however adapted and simplified, are entirely relevant to any vacancy. There are more sophisticated methods of selection available which most employers would only consider for senior appointments. These include:

(a) intelligence/occupational tests
(b) personality testing
(c) psychometric testing
(d) graphology (handwriting assessment)
(e) group assessment centres.

However controversial or expensive some of these systems are, they must be seen only as extra contributions to the overall selection procedure. All relevant facts, factors, behaviour and skills must be collated and compared before getting to the point of making a decision.

The decision

- The human resource manager should assemble all the relevant information on the "short-list" of applicants, including interview notes and the results of any practical tests.
- The relevant manager and supervisor should be involved. The more agreed commitment there is the better.
- There will be subjective arguments and reasons put forward. Question any statements which are not backed up by hard evidence (eg "I didn't like Mr X", "I thought Miss Y was hiding something", "He wouldn't fit in", "She'll want to start a family soon").
- Be aware of any discrimination factors in the decision-making process.
- Ensure personal clarity about the merits and justification for the final selection decision.
- Always consider a reserve candidate. Remember that the person selected might not accept the job.
- Agree the terms of the job offer and get back to the selected candidate as quickly as possible. Any delay could discourage or lose the desired applicant.
- Some hotels take operative staff on initially as casual workers until performance is assessed. Trial periods may also be used.

SKILLS TRAINING

(See also: "Behavioural Training", "Training Plans", "Trainees")

Whether the new recruit is an experienced hospitality worker or brand new to the industry, he or she will require some level of training in the organisation's standards and procedures. If quality of product and service is to be assured to the customer, then the consistent delivery of high standards and the meeting of customer expectations must be a feature of the operation.

Skills training covers both practical skills, such as waiting or technical kitchen abilities, and aspects of social skills as in caring for and greeting the customer.

The overall principle must be to ensure that no member of staff is "let loose" on a customer until he or she has achieved a satisfactory standard of technical, social or behavioural skill.

A systematic approach

Action	How?
1. Assess individual's abilities	Previous experience From interview Induction Head of Department discussion first week "On-job" observation under supervision
2. Plan programme of training	Checklist of skills Plan over "x" no. of weeks Plan who trains Compare standards of performance.
3. Carry out training	Variety of "off-job", "on-job" training under supervision, individually and/or in groups. Training methods to include demonstration, questions, practice in stages and repetition.
4. Reassess individual's abilities	At end of programme use proficiency test, observation and questioning on key skills and standards
5. Refresher training for all	Specific skills and standards re-trained at regular intervals New standards introduced

Implications of systematic approach

- Training must be a line management or supervisory responsibility, which should be clearly noted in their job descriptions.
- Those training, should be *given* training on the best approaches to ensure that their instruction is effective, in results, in time and therefore in cost.

- Achieving the required standard (step 4) could be used as a basis for increasing wage to full rate.
- Assessment of an individual's skills should be regular, and failure to achieve standards or a deterioration should lead to corrective action which may include taking disciplinary measures.
- Skills training is a fundamental part of any quality management effort.
- Skills training must be tailored to the needs of the individual, for example:
  - a youth training recruit
  - an employment training recruit
  - a new recruit to industry
  - a new recruit with experience at a different type of outlet
  - developing skills of existing workers.
- Skills training must always be done bearing in mind the customer, as in reception or food service, and statutory requirements, such as food hygiene and fire precautions legislation.
- The more systematic and the more effective the training, the more successful the business will be.

STAFF HANDBOOK

(See also ''Terms and Conditions'')

Many employee disputes occur because of a lack of information or misunderstandings over unclear rules and procedures. A staff handbook can help to avoid such problems by documenting all the information that should be understood by an employee. It does not have to be an expensively produced item, but could be a simple leaflet or even a typed note. However, its importance as a clear written statement of the firm's policies, rules and regulations cannot be over-stressed. Such a document should be given to staff at induction and they should be encouraged to refer to it regularly.

The actual content of such a handbook will vary according to the size and type of organisation. Larger organisations are now including a full statement of conditions of employment which apply to *all* employees. This may not be practicable in some businesses.

When revising or producing a new staff handbook, the following checklist could be helpful.

Checklist of staff handbook entries

Section A — "Welcome"
Message of welcome by "the boss"
Business description
"Mission statement" of the business
Business history
Any other locations of organisation
Organisation chart
Who's who of staff

Section B — Employment Conditions
Wages/salaries and method of payment
Payment period
Tax, National Insurance and other deductions
Hours of work
Overtime arrangements
Part-time employment
Annual holidays
Holiday period and entitlement
Public holiday arrangements
Unpaid leave
Jury service
Termination of employment
Notice periods
Absence and sickness
Company sickness benefit scheme
Statutory sick pay
Pension arrangements

Section C — Procedures and policies
Fire precautions procedures
Health and safety policy
Food handling and hygiene policy
Equal opportunities policy
Trade union policy
Disciplinary procedures
Dismissal procedures
Grievance and appeal procedures
Maternity leave

Maternity pay and SMP
Training policy
Appraisal procedures
Retirement policy
First aid procedures

Section D — Rules and Regulations
Rules on attendance, absence
Change of address
Accidents procedure
Rules on security (keys, cash, etc)
Safety regulations
Protective clothing
Uniforms, personal appearance
Right of search
Confidential information
Use of firm's property
Removal of firm's property
Personal belongings
Lockers and locker rooms
Lost property
Off-duty rules
Telephone calls
Smoking policy
Drinking, unauthorised drugs
Customer areas
Customer lifts usage
Expenses
Collections and raffles
Statements to media
Time off for doctor/dentist
"Other" employment rules
References on termination
Name badge wearing
Entrances and exits
Staff visitors
Live-in accommodation rules

Section E — Benefits and Amenities
Map or floor plan
Employee restaurant

Medical facilities
Sports and social facilities
Staff noticeboards
Transport facilities, taxis
Parking area
Childcare facility
All other staff benefits:
(eg meals on duty, bereavement leave,
bonuses, staff purchases, discounts)

SUCCESSION PLANNING

Succession planning is about getting the right person in the right job at the right time. Successful managers do it without even thinking. In effect it is "talent spotting". By planning ahead any likely moves of existing personnel, and the training and development of currently less experienced but talented staff, the entire recruitment burden can be substantially eased. This good practice is a key reason why any type of "team" continues to be successful. Football teams do not wait for their players to age and retire or to be tempted by lucrative overseas offers — they spot talent and develop it so that these players can take over in the first team.

Step-by-step succession planning

This should be carried out by the overall senior manager and the human resource manager.

1. Review major business goals.
2. Review the organisation structure for the future.
3. Assess existing employees:
   (a) current performance
   (b) time in job
   (c) time in establishment
   (d) potential
   (e) aims and ambitions.
4. Plan, anticipating possible moves of key personnel.
5. Review the potential of less experienced personnel.
6. Earmark certain people for particular positions.

7. Plan the training and development for those individuals on the succession "ladder". Set objectives and time-scales.

8. A high degree of confidentiality should be maintained but individuals earmarked for development should be motivated by the realisation that the firm has plans for them. However, anything too specific could lead to major problems with other personnel.

9. If a review of current staff reveals that there is nobody in the organisation who could, for example, be trained up to be the restaurant manager in two years, then it is necessary to plan a recruitment strategy or, in a multi-unit company, to find out what talent for future promotion exists elsewhere in the group.

10. No team will last forever. A lack of succession planning due to complacency will suddenly put the business at risk as continuity is broken and the firm hurriedly recruits an unknown quantity to fill a key position.

Succession planning chart

A useful exercise to make job planning visual and more instructive is to extend the organisation chart to include possible successors to each of the key positions. An example of a catering complex is given below. Each "box" on the organisation chart is enlarged to cover more relevant information for planning purposes:

NAME	
JOB	
A	B
C	D

A = Age
B = Time in this job
C = Performance Rating
  (1, 2, 3, 4 where 1 is high)
D = Likely to move rating:
  1 = in next year
  2 = 2 years
  3 = 3 years/never

Following a review of the organisation, and current abilities, the succession planning chart could look like this:

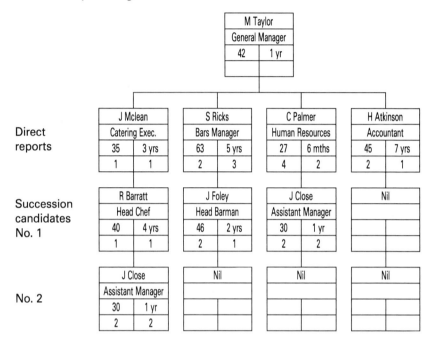

	M Taylor	
	General Manager	
	42	1 yr

Direct reports

J Mclean		S Ricks		C Palmer		H Atkinson	
Catering Exec.		Bars Manager		Human Resources		Accountant	
35	3 yrs	63	5 yrs	27	6 mths	45	7 yrs
1	1	2	3	4	2	2	1

Succession candidates No. 1

R Barratt		J Foley		J Close		Nil	
Head Chef		Head Barman		Assistant Manager			
40	4 yrs	46	2 yrs	30	1 yr		
1	1	2	1	2	2		

No. 2

J Close		Nil		Nil		Nil	
Assistant Manager							
30	1 yr						
2	2						

Points to note

1. J McLean has three years in the job, is performing very well and is likely to move soon. Is the Head Chef ready and trained up? Who will fill the Head Chef's position if he or she does gain promotion?
2. J Close could be a longer-term successor for the Catering Executive role, but could also be an earlier candidate for the Human Resources job.
3. Bars Manager S Ricks is to retire in two years, so will J Foley be able to take over, because if not, there is no further succession candidate.
4. C Palmer, Human Resources, only has six months service and is *not* performing well. If Palmer "does not make it", will J Close be ready to take over? If not, no other candidate is identified.
5. H Atkinson, likely to move in next year, and with a long time in the job already is not covered by any succession candidate. This highlights a priority recruitment or transfer plan.
6. M Taylor, the General Manager, would need to be assessed by the next level of management, unless he or she is the owner, of course! One possibility is that J McLean could be a succession candidate for the General Manager position, or for a similar position in another such unit.

SUPERVISOR TRAINING

The most common path to a supervisory position in any sector of the hospitality industry is from the "shop floor". Employees who are first class operatives and show splendid qualities of reliability and conscientiousness are frequently promoted to a position of supervision over operatives. Thus, the excellent waiter becomes a shift supervisor in the coffee-shop, the efficient chambermaid becomes a floor housekeeper, the reliable barman becomes head barman and so on. This is excellent for career advancement, and the industry should "sell" itself on how many, often quite young, people achieve promotion and career development.

However, often an excellent operative finds the jump too much, becomes disillusioned and leaves rather than risk embarrassment by a "return to the ranks". This is often because a very basic fact has been ignored by the well-meaning manager who promoted the employee. The skills necessary to be a first-class operative are *not* those necessary to be a first-class supervisor. Yet little training is given to such individuals who suddenly find themselves in the midst of the problems of legislation, budgeting and dealing with staff who so recently were their work mates. Many end up wishing they had not accepted promotion.

Promotion to any new level must be associated with training and briefing that covers the new and enhanced skills and procedures which will be crucial aspects of the new job. It is a matter of assessing knowledge and abilities and identifying training needs as if the employee was a new recruit, fresh from induction. This does not have to mean expensive, time-consuming, off-job supervisory training courses, though such experience may be useful. The manager responsible must talk to the individual, discuss the new job description or its priorities and coach the individual by involvement and working together, to the new skills required.

The manager should welcome questions, the need for assurance and confirmation of actions, and be a "safety net" for some considerable time.

If specific training is required, consideration could be given to an open learning package, or a short course at a local college or through the Hotel and Catering Training Company (HCTC).

The checklist below will assist in formulating the basis for the training, coaching and information which should be provided to smooth the way for promotion and supervisory success.

Supervisor training checklist

Section A: Legal aspects

- Staff terms and conditions explained
- supervisory aspects of health and safety
- food hygiene legislation
- fire precautions responsibilities
- licensing laws
- discrimination implications
- disciplinary procedures/authority
- dismissal procedures/authority
- maternity and sickness procedures
- any legislation pertinent to actual position.

Section B: Supervisory knowledge and skills

- Compilation of rotas
- wage control/overtime/casuals
- budget familiarisation
- computer skills needed
- training skills
- development of trainees/staff
- interviewing skills
- selection techniques
- relationship with staff
- social and interpersonal skills
- delegation skills
- communication to staff.

Section C: Managerial skill development

- Communication upwards/feedback
- departmental/management meetings
- business plan familiarisation
- confidentiality and integrity
- handling grievances from staff
- motivational techniques
- counselling techniques
- monitoring performance
- managerial perspective: "no longer one of the boys or girls".

TERMINATION

(See also: "Disciplinary Procedures", "Terms and Conditions", "Emotions", "Redundancy")

Once the disciplinary procedure has been properly implemented but without an improvement in performance or conduct, the final step is to dismiss. Such a step could be summary dismissal following an investigated, confirmed incident of gross misconduct. Every termination must be handled professionally and with serious sensitivity. Be sure that:

(a) there is sufficient reason to dismiss
(b) alternative action has been considered
(c) the firm has acted consistently with prior disciplinary action
(d) there is a belief that the decision to dismiss is fair.

The reasons for dismissal, when fair and reasonable in all the circumstances, are:

(a) *capability*: the employee is unable to do the work or cannot through sickness, or lacks the technical or academic qualifications
(b) *conduct*: when compared to rules and procedures
(c) *redundancy*: when true and fairly selected
(d) *illegitimacy*: eg no work permit or illegal immigrant
(e) *any other substantial reason.*

The termination hearing

The employee must be informed, preferably in writing of the following:

(a) that the meeting will be a disciplinary hearing
(b) the time and place (specifically)
(c) the right to be accompanied by a fellow employee
(d) exactly who will represent the company, eg manager with dismissal authority and personnel manager.

The meeting must obviously be very serious, private and uninterrupted. The line manager should lead and announce the decision. The sequence at the meeting could be as follows:

(a) previous meetings and action reviewed
(b) particular attention directed to the last disciplinary hearing where the possibility of dismissal was clearly stated
(c) before the decision is announced, the employee should be given the opportunity to add anything to previous statements
(d) the line manager should confirm that as for example, there has been no improvement in performance, the decision is that the person's employment with the organisation is to be terminated
(e) the person should be informed of the effective date of termination dependant on whether the notice period is to be worked or paid in lieu
(f) the personnel manager should be prepared to itemise all other termination details, such as holiday pay, pension arrangements, return of company property such as uniform, credit cards, even company car
(g) it should also be stated that all these details will be confirmed in writing and the P45 sent in due course
(h) the individual still retains the right of appeal, which should be put in writing within five working days. (This also applies in summary dismissal cases.)
(i) the personnel manager should ask if the individual has any questions, and this can include the accompanying fellow employee
(j) behaviour should be calm, firm and concerned
(k) employees with two years' service may request "written reasons for dismissal", to be provided within 14 days. Such a statement must be clear and accurate as it could be used at any subsequent industrial tribunal.

Types of termination

1. *Resignation*
   The employee gives notice to the employer in line with the terms and conditions of employment. As such, the employee has not been dismissed and may not claim unfair dismissal. However, if forced by circumstances to resign (see below) a claim of "constructive dismissal" may be lodged.
2. *Dismissal with notice*
   The employer gives notice to the employee that the contract of employment will terminate at the expiry of the notice. The period

of notice to be worked will be as in the terms and conditions of employment, or payment may be made in lieu of working the notice — often the most sensible outcome for the rest of the workforce. Payment in lieu must cover the value of all fringe benefits that would have been enjoyed in the notice period, such as private medical insurance payments. Where notice periods are not stated, minimum legal periods must be observed: one week for four weeks' service to two years, increasing by one week for every year of service up to a maximum of 12.

With regard to notice periods it is also necessary to consider the following issues:

(a) whilst a notice period elapses, all other terms of the employment contract must still apply
(b) notice is effective only when it has been *received*. A letter of dismissal sent while the employee is away would delay the effective date of termination.
(c) notice, once given by either employer or employee cannot be withdrawn unless by total mutual consent.
(d) "heat of the moment" resignations or dismissals may be retracted if action is taken quickly to follow proper procedure.

Dismissal without notice

Where gross misconduct has taken place, the contract is deemed to have been repudiated or destroyed, and as a result summary dismissal will follow. There is no period of notice nor payment in lieu, and holiday pay entitlement is also withheld.

Wrongful dismissal

This is:

(a) where the proper notice period is not given or
(b) no payment is made in lieu of notice or
(c) holiday pay, sick pay or other entitlements are improperly withheld, and note that
(d) the burden of proof is on the employer, and such dismissal is
(e) a civil court matter.

Unfair Dismissal

Unfair dismissal may be claimed where the employee:

(a) has completed two years or more continuous service
(b) works 16 hours or more per week
(c) works eight hours or more per week with five years or more service
(d) is not above normal retirement age (65 unless otherwise stated by the company)
(e) is dismissed due to being a member of an independent trade union
(f) is dismissed due to taking part in independent trade union activities
(g) is dismissed for not being a member of such a trade union
(h) is dismissed due to pregnancy
(i) is dismissed without proper recourse to disciplinary procedures and the code of practice.

(See also "Industrial Tribunals")

Constructive dismissal

The employee resigns due to a breach of contract by the employer or unreasonable treatment and behaviour by the employer.

(a) The breach must be a serious matter (eg lower wages, different hours of work).
(b) The employee must leave.
(c) The employee must leave soon after the initial breach.
(d) The courts will consider the circumstances against the implied common law duty of trust and good faith, eg if an employee leaves as a result of being reprimanded in an insulting fashion in front of other staff and customers, or if a company gives an employee one week's notice of moving job to a distant location within the organisation, or if wages paid have been below the minimum set by a Wages Council Order.

Termination settlement (ACAS settlement)

In the case mainly of senior employees, termination may be by mutual agreement of the parties. Such settlements include a termination package of severance or ex-gratia payments and other benefits which nowadays may include career counselling and sponsored "outplacement", where an agency finds an alternative job for the outgoing individual. Such arrangements will normally be "rubber-stamped" by the Advisory Conciliation and Arbitration Service (ACAS).

Exit interviewing

Every termination procedure, with the exception of summary dismissal, should include an exit interview. This is best carried out by the person responsible for human resources, as the most impartial member of management and therefore the most likely to get the departing worker to be frank and open.

Exit interviews can be an opportunity simply to "moan", but on occasion they can also reveal vital facts, trends and inside information about employment and management practices.

It is for the human resources manager to take note of what is said or implied, record the interview and decide on the most positive and constructive action to take.

A format for an exit interview is contained in Appendix 2. Also in Appendix 2, is a pro forma for a leaver's form for internal use, and a checklist to ensure that all termination details and actions have been completed.

TERMS AND CONDITIONS

(See also "Induction", "Staff Handbook")

At the moment when an employee accepts a job offer, there is a contract of employment between the parties. A verbal agreement based on the simple job offer, and details of the wages to be paid and the job to be done is legally binding. However, as with so much in employment, if the terms of the contract are clearly written and communicated, there will be less chance of misunderstanding and conflict.

When the employee actually commences employment the basic terms and conditions of employment should be communicated as discussed in "Induction". This may be in the form of one all-encompassing contractual document or it may be a combination of conditions outlined in the job offer letter, a statement of terms and conditions, and in the staff handbook. In any case, the following legal entitlement must be observed:

(a) it is a requirement that employers must provide a written statement of terms and conditions within 13 weeks of the commencement of the employment
(b) this applies to employees working 16 hours or more per week, or those working eight hours or more per week with five years' service.

Written statement of terms and conditions

Regardless of the size of the operation, it is necessary to clarify the contractual relationship between the firm and an employee by itemising the following details:

(a) the firm's name
(b) the employee's name
(c) date of starting work
(d) date from which continuous service began
(e) job title
(f) the wage to be paid
(g) how often the wage will be paid (weekly or monthly)
(h) the hours of work
(i) holiday entitlement
(j) sickness and pension details
(k) notice period on either side
(l) disciplinary rules (20 + employees)
(m) grievance and appeal details.

Implied terms

Such items are described as the "express terms" of the contract. In addition there are duties under common law which imply further terms and which will be recognised by the courts. These include:

(a) maintenance of trust and confidence through cooperation
(b) both parties to act in good faith
(c) the taking of reasonable care to ensure health and safety for all in the workplace

(d) the employee must obey lawful and reasonable orders and not commit misconduct

(e) the employer must pay the agreed wage and provide work when available

(f) the employer must not require the employee to commit an unlawful act

(g) implied terms can also arise out of practices that have developed over time; these are known as "custom and practice"

(h) implied terms can also arise through changes in the firm's rules, which must be notified to the employee

(i) none of the statutory rights, from equal pay to maternity benefits to statutory sick pay, can be waived by the express terms and conditions of employment.

Changes in terms and conditions

Employees must be informed within one month of the introduction of a change in terms and conditions. In practice, such matters should be discussed with employees. The firm should obtain their consent and get them to sign a slip of paper outlining the change to their written statement of terms and conditions. Such documentation could be vital in any future disagreement over employment rights.

- When taking over another business, continuous service will be calculated from the date that employees joined the previous owner. This has great bearing on employment rights and should be clear in the contract.
- Hospitality units should clarify the right to search employees.
- Live-in accommodation arrangements should be clearly stated, including the procedures on termination of employment.
- The hourly rate of pay for overtime, part-time, and the termination pay calculations should be clear.
- Holiday periods and entitlement are often a point of confusion. Prepare a table based on length of service and annual entitlement and a table showing holiday entitlement dependent on month of starting and holiday pay dependent on the month of an employee leaving (format in Appendix 2).
- The rate of payment for working on Bank and Public Holidays (normally double time and a day off in lieu) should be confirmed.

TRAINEES

(See also "Industrial Release Placements", "Young People")

The hospitality industry has made tremendous efforts in the last few years to improve its image as an employer. It has tackled the lack of interest in this sector shown by school leavers nationally. By encouraging more young people to choose a career in one of its many job areas it can ensure the quality of the potential workforce of the future.

Trainees are not all young people, and it is necessary to be aware of the large numbers of more mature individuals who are now finding a second career in the service sector.

For these reasons the industry's approach to people on training schemes of any type or people just learning a new set of skills and knowledge, must be thorough and responsible. Trainees are the future labour pool, and traumatic experiences at an early stage in their careers will influence them for all time.

Trainees need to contribute, and learn the business, with all its unpredictability and pressure. They should not be cocooned in a rigid, manual-based training programme. They need to experience the real world, and they need to enjoy its dynamism and variety.

Types of trainees

Government training schemes

Youth Training (YT) and Employment Training (ET) have existed for a while, and are now controlled through the Training and Enterprise Councils or Local Enterprise Councils in Scotland. The Government guarantees a YT place for every person between 16 and 18 years old who wants one. The cost of employing a YT trainee is funded by government, up to 50 per cent. It is a two year programme, including 20 weeks' off-job training. Administratively it can be cumbersome, and some leading employers such as Midland Bank and Mothercare have pulled out of the scheme for this reason. However, YT is important to the hospitality industry, and most trainees are under the managing agency of the Hotel and Catering Training Company which, through the Caterbase scheme, can award a National Vocational Qualification (NVQ) certificate on successful completion.

ET is geared to the longer-term unemployed and has been a useful vehicle for women to re-enter the labour market. It is important to note that YT and ET trainees count as full employees when assessing the headcount for legal reasons such as health and safety procedures.

Apprentices

This status is mostly confined to chefs on City and Guilds apprenticeships, inclusive of a day or block release at college. It is a high status apprenticeship which requires the kitchen brigade to be training oriented and to have some training qualification.

Departmental trainees

Many young people enter specific job areas, for example, the restaurant or reception and even if they have had some formal training, such as a reception course at a college of further education, they will still require an on-job training programme to turn theory into everyday practice.

Management trainees

Management trainees may be on a specific in-company programme, monitored and organised by a central human resource function or may possibly be in-house trainees, "talent-spotted" by the management as having management potential. Their training programmes will tend to be longer and move from operative know-how to specialist functions and management skills.

College work experience

Most further and higher education courses in the hospitality area require students to undertake a period of supervised work experience. This can vary from a few weeks as part of a one year receptionist course, to a whole year's placement for a degree level undergraduate. This work experience placement is crucial in further convincing students that they have made the right career choice. It can also influence which sector they will choose on completion of their course.

Industrial release placements are covered specifically elsewhere in this book.

Management of trainees

Management of trainees should be through a step by step approach:

1. Agree with line management and supervisors the types and numbers of trainees to be recruited.
2. Agree the budget, the wage costs and the phasing of such costs with the accountant.
3. Plan the "trainee" year, phasing placements from colleges so that there are not too many at one time. Consider specific trading peaks and troughs through the year, and the varying business volume of departments eg trainees in banqueting are not needed in the summer.
4. Establish and maintain strong liaison links with colleges, industrial placement tutors, careers services, the local HCTC, the local Training and Enterprise Council, and Job Centres, all of which can provide trainee candidates.
5. Each trainee should be properly recruited and selected. Do not take anyone without an interview for very soon they will be representing the organisation.
6. Each trainee recruited should have a written programme containing the overall objective of the training period, an outline of the departments to be covered, dates (subject to change) and any off-job training elements. This forms a "learning agreement" between the firm and the trainee.
7. A progress review and assessment method should be built into the system.
8. All involved managers and heads of department, and the department supervisors and trainers of each trainee's programme should be fully briefed. Each department should have reminders about their next trainee's start date and objectives. Personnel should ensure that everyone is happy with the time spent in each department; if it is too short it could be a disincentive to train properly or may be impractical as so much has to be learnt to be proficient.
9. Towards the end of a trainee's programme assessments and appraisal should also question the vital issue of whether there will be a permanent job offer for the individual.

TRAINING PLANS

(See also: "Induction", "Skills Training", "Trainees")

Training is more likely to happen and to be supported and implemented by line management if it is planned systematically in full coordination with all areas of the business. Simply speaking, it should be totally driven by the needs of the business (indeed, by the training element of the business plan). The training plan must also be a practical working document. It must be flexible and able to react to changes in priority within an ever-dynamic business scenario.

Training plans may be formulated at three distinct levels:

(a) *The individual*
This involves personalised identified training needs, such as the head chef needs training on man-management and budget control.
(b) *Departmental*
This involves the specific needs of certain work groups, eg receptionists need training on the new computerised front desk system.
(c) *All staff*
Training is required across the board, eg induction, fire training, health and safety, social skills.

Plan and be proactive

Much of the above can be planned well in advance; indeed the human resources manager should look a year ahead and anticipate events, needs and priorities so that these can be approached systematically and not with last-minute training "frenzies".

● It is relatively easy to plan much of the legal or statutory training where specific timescales apply. For example, fire training has to be carried out every six months for all staff, and every three months for night or live-in personnel.
● Some training should be planned for specific times of the year, such as pre-season training, energy-saving instruction before winter and training prior to Christmas and other "specials".

- Training should be planned in line with peaks and troughs; do not arrange sessions for all staff during the busiest part of the year.
- Trainees should be taken on at different times of the year, not all at once, and not when supervisors are too busy to train effectively.
- In liaison with line management refresher training sessions on such matters as social skills, customer care and operating expenses reduction should be pre-planned throughout the year.
- Major training priorities must be taken from the major business plan objectives and planned to be effective and timely. Examples could be the introduction of a new menu or service style, installation of new systems and equipment, or the upgrading of the hotel from three to four star, or a major improvement in customer care.
- If there is a need to use external training courses then this must be planned for and places booked. Again, check that the dates of the training do not conflict with business volume forecasts.

Be flexible and reactive

Training managers lose credibility when they are not seen to be contributing directly towards business priorities and problems. Training plans should be changed if demanded by needs and situations.

- Do not be over-ambitious with the plan; build in some "slack" for unplanned occurrences, those inevitable issues which suddenly assume enormous significance.
- Be aware of operational problems and react quickly and positively.
- Prioritise the plan so that essential elements are clearly identified and the important, but not totally essential items which may be postponed, are recognised as such.
- Compile a "published" plan on a quarterly basis so that achievements and outstanding matters can be reviewed before the next quarter.

Formulating training plans

- Training plans must be put together with the full involvement of all line managers and supervisors. They will be doing much of the training and need to be committed to the plan and then guided and "cajoled" by the human resource manager to ensure it happens.
- On a quarterly basis, if appropriate, each supervisor or head of department should submit a plan for their area of work. These departmental plans must be agreed by the line manager responsible, before being coordinated by the human resource manager into an overall business training plan.
- The human resource manager should ensure that his or her senior manager has full input into the plan by requesting comments and additions, based on his or her own business objectives. The senior manager should "sign off" the plan.
- Ensure that he or she knows the cost element of the plan and agrees with budgeting, phasing and amounts.
- Distribute copies of the finished quarterly training plan to all those involved, including staff, and post a copy on the staff noticeboard if appropriate.
- When reviewing the successes and failures of each plan, analyse the reasons, review priorities and use the plans as an opportunity for self-evaluation and an assessment of the departmental supervisors' commitment to training. Wherever possible evaluate the training in terms of financial benefit.

Training plan format

The example below is a quarterly plan for a large contract catering operation. The completion date column is the date by which the training, even if not carried out on the "proposed dates", must be completed. The cost column is left blank as this will depend on localised factors, but remember that if staff are being trained during "paid working hours" then there is a cost (or investment), even though the trainer is an employee rather than an external consultant. For evaluation purposes, readers may wish to add a column for "return on investment".

Example

PORTLAND COMPONENTS PLC

CATERING DIVISION: TRAINING PLAN Apr, May, June '91

Topic	To attend	Trainers	Proposed dates	Completion date	Cost
Waiting Skills Refresher	All Waiting Staff	Restaurants Manager	Apr 15/ 16/17	Apr 30	
New Menu (Begins 1st May)	All Staff	Training Officer General Manager	Apr 22-25	Apr 30	
Food Hygiene Certificates	50% Kitchen 50% Rest.	HCTC External	May 15/16	May 16	
New Recipes	Chefs	Head Chef	Apr 20-30	Apr 30	
Stores Control	Storeman	Head Chef	May 25	June 15	
Beverage Service	2 Commis Waiters	Restaurants Supervisor	May 18/19	June 30	
Cashiering	New Cashier (DOS Apr 5)	Accountant	Apr 5-7	Apr 7	
Fire Precautions	All Staff	Training Officer	June 7/ 14/21	June 30	
Budgetary Control	Head Chef Restaurants Manager	General Manager	May 6	May 10	

VACANCY

(See also: "Recruitment", "Labour Market", "Succession Planning")

When a vacancy arises, whether it is known about for some time or not, the natural reaction is to attempt replacement with an identikit individual: the same type of person, on the same terms and conditions (or slightly less if possible), the same organisation, job role and duties. By avoiding this "knee-jerk" reaction, and by using some lateral thinking, it is possible to consider a vacancy as a very positive opportunity to review the situation and perhaps make some changes.

When a vacancy arises consider the following reactions:

(a) review strategy and business plan
(b) review the organisation structure
(c) review the job description
(d) review the person specification
(e) investigate alternative methods of operation
(f) think about revising the way current staff are used
(g) *speak* to customers, and *listen* to them.

Such a process should provide answers to the following questions:

(a) Does a vacancy exist?
(b) What exactly is the vacancy?
(c) How should the vacancy be filled?

When considering the methods of filling a vacancy, ask searching questions such as:

(a) Does this business need a Food and Beverage Manager, an Assistant Food and Beverage Manager, a Restaurant Manager, a Head Chef and a Bars Manager?
(b) Is a Restaurant Manager replacement needed when the two supervisors could share the job under management supervision?
(c) Could two local, committed, and stable part-timers share this previously single person full-time job?
(d) Could first level staff be given more responsibilities, be more involved, and therefore reduce the need for a level of relatively non-productive, high-cost middle management?
(e) What does the customer want?

WAGES

(See also: "Terms and Conditions", "Productivity", "Rotas")

The hospitality industry is nervous and touchy about discussion of wages. Its reputation with the general public is that of a low pay sector. Often this is unfair as many employers have made steady but consistent improvement in terms and conditions. Recent surveys have certainly supported the view that there is a healthy trend in this area. However, the image of the industry and its attraction to potential employees is still being tarnished by a number of employers who pay wages below the Wages Council minimum and, in addition, provide very poor conditions.

A recent Low Pay Unit survey found many firms paying below the minimum. There are non-wage benefits such as tips, meals, accommmodation, and therefore inter-industry comparisons of wages alone may not look favourable and may not be entirely fair.

Wage costs are a very large item of expenditure for many firms — from around 10 per cent of sales in pubs to 20-30 per cent in hotels and restaurants. The management of wages must involve a balanced approach between fair rates, the motivation of staff through performance-related pay, and full control of this major expense.

Both the HCIMA and the BHA offer members a salaries and wages advisory service.

Legal and good practice issues

- The Wages Council Order sets a minimum hourly rate, overtime rate and a maximum deduction for live-in accommodation. This does not apply to employees under 21 years of age.

  Minimum rates at the time of writing are: cafe and unlicensed — £2.80 per hour, hotels and restaurants — £2.50 per hour, and pubs and clubs — £2.80 per hour.
- Each employee must be provided with an itemised pay statement, identifying the gross wage, fixed and variable deductions, and the net wage.
- The employee must give consent for any further deductions beyond National Insurance and PAYE.
- The written statement of terms and conditions of employment should very clearly confirm:

- — hourly rate (or salary)
- — overtime rates
- — holiday pay entitlement
- — sick pay entitlement
- — public holiday premium rates.

- The Equal Pay Act demands equality of pay between men and women for like work of like value.
- It is necessary to be clear about the week or five working days "in hand" system which is still common in the hospitality sector. The first five working days are only paid for on termination in many firms.
- It is necessary to be clear as to whether or not various staff categories are actually paid for breaks, whether for meals or refreshment.
- Clear guidance should be given on the distribution of tips and gratuities which can be a source of misunderstanding, grievance, and outright conflict.
- The firm's policy on "subs" (advances on wages) should be stated. Generally, these should be avoided totally.
- The payment system should be fair to long-service staff, and they should not be upset by the arrival of newcomers on the same or higher wages.
  Remuneration systems should recognise and reward long service, especially in a high labour-turnover business.
- Payment by credit transfer should be encouraged. This helps security by avoiding large money collections from the bank on pay day.

Wage control

- The overall responsibility for wage control must be that of the senior line manager, assisted perhaps by the human resources manager or wages clerk.
- The administration of wages should be carried out by a wages clerk, responsible to the accountant in larger businesses.
- The firm or each department of a larger organisation must have clear departmental responsibility for wage control, including the submission of time sheets.
- Wage control must be based on weekly sales forecasts. Such information should be issued by the manager or accountant so

that the line person responsible can assess the level of staffing required. Ideally this should be on the basis of known productivity norms but a "finger in the air" may be necessary in some cases.

Wage forecasts can be drawn up and staff rotas and organisation must then reflect the forecast. Rotas should be checked regularly by personnel for efficiency and anomalies.

● All overtime and casual payments must be authorised by the management. There should be a full explanation accompanying the request for authorisation. This requirement for prior authorisation encourages labour planning.

● Larger businesses may use a computerised payroll system which can provide a range of analyses, reports and information. Firms may be contracted to provide the service, which can include assistance in making up the pay packets. This service costs, at the time of writing, a minimum of £300 per month.

Example

A wage system

The following procedure is given as a guide for a review of the wages system. It is for an hotel business with 50 full-time staff; a computerised payroll input service is contracted out.

1. Departmental time sheets are completed and given to the wages clerk by 10.30 am on Monday morning.
2. The total work hours are calculated per employee.
3. Time-sheets are authorised by the General Manager. Hours in excess of the basic hours require full supporting documentation.
4. The General Manager questions heads of department on excess hours and casual payments.
5. The wages clerk enters additional payments due on to the computerised input sheet; much of the information, such as name and basic wage, is already input.
6. Various payments are entered under the relevant codes, eg SSP, holiday pay, lieu days.

7. The total holiday pay is entered gross though the tax and NI figures are calculated on the basic weekly wage (not the lump sum). Basic wages are suspended for the holiday period.

8. Any leavers are entered; the computer system will calculate P45 details and issue a P45.

9. All input sheets are photocopied to handle queries.

10. The total weekly wage cost to the hotel is calculated by the true figure spent and the employer's NI contributions.

11. The whole is posted by special delivery to the payroll company, to arrive Tuesday morning.

12. On Wednesday, reports on tax, NI, SSP, maternity pay, a departmental wages analysis and so on are received from the payroll company. Also, empty wage packets with pre-printed itemised pay statements are received. "Dummy" wage packets and payslips are also sent.

13. On Thursday the wage reports and figures are submitted to Head Office.

14. On Friday the petty cash vouchers total is added to the wages total. Money is ordered from the bank — the computer payroll will itemise the notes and coins required. The General Manager and wages clerk go at various times, in taxis from various companies, to the bank for the collection of money. Special arrangements are made regarding the collection point. The wage packets are completed and distributed on Friday afternoon. Those which are not collected are given to the duty manager and placed in the main safe. All wages must be signed for by the relevant member of staff.

YOUNG PEOPLE

The significance of young people to the hotel and catering industry cannot be overstressed. A typical staff profile analysis may reveal that 50 per cent of the total workforce is aged 25 or under and yet surveys still show that very few school leavers consider the hospitality industry as a preferred career choice. This attitude is changing slowly as parents, teachers and the children themselves become more aware of the dominance of service industries as a whole. Demographic discussions of the past few years tend to influence us into believing that the labour market will be older, and increasingly female. However we must not lose sight of the importance of attracting school and college leavers, many of whom change their minds about a hospitality career after a negative industrial placement experience.

The legal restrictions on the employment of young people have been eased since 1989. There are now no specific legal constraints on the hours of work given to 16 to 18-year-olds (formerly termed "young persons" in law). However, no child under 13 years of age may be employed under the conditions below:

(a) before 7 am or after 7 pm
(b) before close of school
(c) more than two hours on a school day
(d) more than two hours on Sunday
(e) to lift, carry or move such heavy objects that injury could result.

This latter point highlights employers' special responsibility for health and safety at work. Unfortunately, for example, training schemes such as YTS and Youth Training (YT) have been dogged by poor safety records. Employers must ensure that supervision is close, and experienced, and be mindful of the lack of worldly experience and judgement of even the most mature-looking 17-year-old.

Understanding young people

Generations of youngsters differ greatly in their experience, perception and expectation. They are employed by people who are products of a different life-style and experience. The key to successful employment of young people is to try and understand them better, anticipate their expectations, and integrate the outcome of this exercise into job designs, training and methods of management.

A fascinating, long-term study of a particular generation is "Youthscan". This project is monitoring how 15,000 people born in one week in 1970 are developing. Some of the findings and, more significantly, the implications of these results are of interest to employers in the hospitality business. For example:

(a) French was seen as one of the *least* useful subjects
(b) 70 per cent *had* attended careers advice sessions
(c) 77 per cent *had* attended talks by industry representatives
(d) one in three *had* had some work experience
(e) only 3.5 per cent indicated a career preference for the catering industry (this includes the "food" industry).

There are very clear signals here with implications for human resource strategy recruitment campaigns, schools liaison, school talks and visits, language training and the availability of work experience. In other words, we must try to assess the overall motivation of today's young people and attempt to take some measures to satisfy and accommodate these drives and expectations.

A pause for optimism

The "Youthscan" study has one major finding of real and genuine optimism for the hospitality industry. The data reveals that "caring for others" rates very highly on this group's scale of values. Such a factor could have splendid outcomes for all service industries, and for the hospitality business in particular. It is worth a fresh look at strategic and tactical plans for young people to make sure that the individual business gets its share of the *best*.

Part 3
ISSUES AT WORK

ABSENTEEISM

(See also: "Alcohol", "Sickness", "Stress")

Absence from work is a significant and costly factor which can greatly reduce productivity and a business' overall profitability. The causes may be perfectly legitimate sickness, properly certificated and requiring concern and sensitivity from the employer. Yet the really damaging forms of absenteeism are the short-term, uncertified causes — the "occasional day-off syndrome", and simple lateness for work.

The costs and operational difficulties caused by this absenteeism can be very damaging. Management must monitor sensibly all absences on an individual and departmental basis. All cases must be treated specifically, within an overall pattern identified over a period of time. Subsequent action may range from medical help, to individual counselling, to disciplinary action. The approach should be analytical and direct:

(a) the absence could be plain malingering
(b) there may be unstated causes for absence excused by "flu" or a "stomach upset"
(c) there may be a regular, yet legitimate cause
(d) there may be a work-related cause.

Each employee should be monitored so that any pattern of absence may be identified. Rather than very occasional longer absences it is the regular day-off pattern which should cause most concern. It could be due to sheer lack of commitment (an employee who decides to pursue the pleasure ethic rather than the work ethic). Alternatively, the real reason, such as work-related stress, personal problems or alcohol abuse may be covered up by claims of sickness.

There are problems which people may experience on a regular, but short-term basis — backache and pre-menstrual syndrome are two of the most common. A pattern may be identified regarding business and work-related activities. Systems at work, periods of high pressure and the style of management are all possible reasons for absenteeism.

Absenteeism analysis

- Each employee should have an absence record.
- Each department, if in a larger organisation, should be monitored and compared with others.
- Absenteeism must be put into quantifiable measures and costs, and these facts presented to line people responsible for action.
- "Lost time" may be calculated in the following way:
$$\frac{\text{total absence in period (hours or days)}}{\text{possible total hours or days available}} \times 100 = \text{lost time rate}$$
- The cost of "lost time" may be calculated by multiplying the average hourly or daily labour cost by the lost time rate.

Procedure for dealing with the "occasional day off"

- Record all absences or lateness and identify any pattern or regularity by individual and department.
- When concerned by a pattern, discuss the issue with the supervisor or manager responsible directly for the individual or department.
- Arrange to speak privately with the individual immediately when he or she returns to work — concern *must* be evident and considerable.
- Counsel the individual by asking questions about health and medical history, based on concern about the recent number of days off.
- Agree with the employee some form of action, such as further chats, a visit to the firm's doctor for a check-up, or a personal plan to improve attendance.
- Personal action plans may often concern a life-style question. Hospitality employees tend to play hard and work hard. The pressure of the work may often lead to excessive smoking and alcohol consumption after work. "Partying" after late shifts in discos and clubs is common and will inevitably lead to "morning after" problems.

- If a lack of commitment or care towards work is identified or there is a continued refusal to attempt improvement, disciplinary action may be necessary. This "jolt" may be what is necessary with some employees to get them back on the tracks.

ACCIDENTS

The facts

- A recent report shows that service industries, including hotel and catering, have experienced an alarming rate of increase in accidents at work — in 1990 14 per cent up over 1989.
- There are 600 deaths per year due to accidents at work.
- There are 400,000 accidents every year that result in absence of more than three days.
- There is a startling lack of qualified first aiders in the hospitality industry, yet many ailments, such as heart attack, need vital treatment within three minutes — well before an ambulance is likely to arrive.

The law

- All accidents at work must be fully recorded (see below). An accident book must be kept and all employees informed where it is, for immediate completion.
- Accidents should be recorded on Form F2509, available from HMSO and booksellers.
- Serious accidents which result in death and injury of a serious nature requiring hospitalisation, whether involving employees or customers, must be reported to the Environmental Health Officer (EHO). Dangerous occurrences or serious incidents which happened without injury must also be reported to the Environmental Health Officer.

Methods of reporting accidents

- The accident book is the easiest method available to provide as much detail as possible.

- Companies may require a more detailed report, for insurance and liability reasons.
- The importance of ensuring that *all* accidents are reported and recorded as near to the time as possible must be stressed to all employees.
- Many industrial injury claims are decided upon the accuracy and detail of the original report.

Example of an accident report
(could also be used for "incidents")

To be completed within 24 hours.
(Immediate details to be recorded in Accident Book.)

Name of person completing report:

Signature:

Date: Time Reported:

Name of injured person:

Address:

Age: DoB:

Department: Sex:

Status if not an employee:

Part of body injured (state left or right):

Details of injury:

Witnesses.

Name, address and place of work:

1.   2.

Date of accident:

Time of accident:

Exact location:

Description of accident:
(Full description of what happened, using extra paper if necessary, iillustrated with sketches/plans where appropriate.)

Analysis of accidents records

- Accidents are very costly in time lost, in productivity, in upset, and on sick pay schemes. Analysis may show recurring reasons for certain accidents.
- Look for patterns, trends, locations and departments with frequent accidents.

- Take management decisions to eradicate accidents; for example, instituting safer working systems, rectifying design faults, repairing or discarding dangerous equipment, and promoting training.

Review of first aid arrangements

- There should be a minimum of one trained, qualified first aider per 50 employees.
- Who are the first aiders? Where are they? How can they be contacted? Ensure that everyone knows who the first aiders are and how and where they can be contacted.
- Ensure that first aiders undergo refresher training regularly (at least every three years), and make sure that first aid supplies are maintained properly.
- Consider bonus payments to qualified first aiders.
- All duty management should be suitably qualified, especially in hotels, where they are invariably the first people on the scene.

AIDS

Much of the fear and "hype" about AIDS stems from ignorance. Every employer should put this right, whilst taking sensible precautionary steps in certain areas of work. Larger firms should formulate a policy statement on AIDS and HIV. The following pointers should help to guide an approach to this important issue facing employment today and in the forseeable future.

- AIDS stands for Acquired Immune Deficiency Syndrome.
- HIV stands for Human Immunodeficiency Virus.
- About 10 per cent of people with the HIV positive condition develop AIDS (*Health and Employment* ACAS advisory booklet).
- There is no danger from an HIV positive person in normal social or work contact.
- The virus is spread by unprotected sexual intercourse, the penetration of the blood stream by infected blood or semen, or by the use of infected hypodermic needles.
- Employees with AIDS or HIV should, by Government guidance, be treated as any other employees, including with regard to

sickness and their physical ability to do the work for which they are contracted.

- Employment rights are not affected, and there must be no discriminatory actions.
- Testing is expensive, often inconclusive and would achieve little. Health questionnaires including AIDS or HIV enquiries are also likely to be of little use.
- As with any medical situation, employers have no right to know the results of medical examinations.
- There are risks at work for some hospitality people, where there is an outside chance of infected blood or semen entering their bloodstream. Room maids, for example, could be issued with protective handgloves for handling used sheets, cleaning hand basins, toilets and so on.
- First aiders may also be at risk and must be warned and issued with protective gloves.
- All employees with cuts and abrasions must be told to cover the wound adequately with an appropriate dressing.
- All employees should be informed of the above facts as a part of their regular health and safety training. *Do not* make a big issue out of such briefings, but state the facts seriously as an integral part of health and safety procedures and instructions.
- If an employee says that he or she is HIV positive or has AIDS, treat the matter with the utmost sensitivity and confidentiality. Ensure that the individual does not broadcast the fact; monitor closely the person's health and if his or her ability to work seems affected, consult his or her doctor, with consent of course.
- For the basis of an AIDS/HIV policy, consult the ACAS booklet *Health and Employment*.
- Further information and advice is available from:
  - **The National Aids Helpline (freephone)**
    0800 555777 for information and literature
    0800 567123 for personal, confidential advice
  - **The Terence Higgins Trust**
    BM/AIDS
    London WC1N 3XX
    071 833 2971
  - **HCIMA Technical Brief on AIDS**

ALCOHOL

The consumption of alcoholic beverages is an integral part of most sectors of the hospitality industry. The people who work in such establishments are subjected to the poor drinking habits of some customers, to temptation all around, and to sustained pressure on duty which may lead to a alcohol-assisted unwinding off duty. All industries have to tackle the problems created by alcohol consumption, including absenteeism, illness, low productivity and performance, and accidents caused by workers under the influence of this "drug".

- The Health Education Authority estimates that £17 billion is lost in low productivity due to alcohol.
- 14 million days are lost every year for reasons and absences connected with alcohol.
- 213 people die every year in an alcoholic stupor.
- Woman suffer problems related to alcohol just as much as men. It is a fact that a woman has only half the enzyme that breaks down alcohol when compared with a man. Hence, the worry over drinking when pregnant.

Set an example

It is essential that employers set visible and consistent examples on alcohol consumption. How many managers have one too many when "entertaining"? Is this the example for employees to see when the firm's disciplinary procedure says that drinking on duty or being "under the influence of alcohol at work" are offences of gross misconduct leading to summary dismissal? Policies on alcohol must be consistent and apply to everyone.

Many organisations have now banned alcohol consumption at boardroom level, including the entertainment of visitors and at company dinners. Large employers which support this policy include ICI, ESSO, P & O, Courtaulds, British Airways and IBM. Training courses are other occasions when restrictions should be imposed on the amount of alcohol consumed.

Business approach to alcohol issues

- Agree clear rules on the use of alcohol.

- Introduce awareness of the issue at induction, life-style training sessions or as a part of the regular health and safety instruction.
- Treat a person's alcohol problem as an illness, needing advice, treatment and counselling.
- Be aware of the alcoholic's "cover-ups"; absenteeism on a regular basis, getting others to call in giving excuses for absence; and physical manifestations such as shaking hands, fatigue and listlessness. Poor performance is another possible indicator.
- Encourage people to seek help and guidance.
- If involved in counselling, try to discover the underlying reasons for perhaps a sudden increase in consumption. Stress, pressure, personal difficulties and unhappiness in the job can all be root causes.
- Disciplinary action, notably summary dismissal for drunkeness at work, may be invoked, but even in such a case it is necessary to assess each individual, and consider his or her past record and length of service.
- If an employee is discovered drinking on duty or under the influence of alcohol, he or she must be suspended immediately and sent home. The employee should be interviewed as soon as possible. It is at this stage that management must decide, considering all the circumstances, what action to take. In practice, there can only be very exceptional cases where dismissal can be avoided because it is necessary to set an example for all other employees.
- Management must seriously consider their own drinking behaviour whilst on the premises. "Mine hosts", accepting every drink offered, may be doing the health of the business as much damage as their own.
- For further information, contact the Health Education Authority (address in Appendix 3).

BEREAVEMENT

Managing people effectively embraces the importance of responding appropriately to their worst and most personal problems. The death of a partner, close relative or friend is just such a situation. Sympathetic reaction is clearly called for; compassionate leave and immediate assistance are suitable gestures from the firm, including a note of condolence and perhaps a wreath or representation at the funeral.

Even more crucial to managing the person through the crisis is the empathy involved in helping the individual when back at work.

Everyone is different and some may find that throwing themselves into thought-consuming work is the best therapy. A sensitive manager must closely, but not obviously, monitor progress, always prepared for a sudden delayed reaction. Depression, stress and downright unhappiness may reach a peak well after the bereavement itself. It is at this stage that a break or holiday may be most valuable; some experts believe this may often be about six months after the initial trauma.

Best practices

- In a 1988 survey carried out by the Institute of Personnel Management, 77 per cent of employers involved gave between one and five days' compassionate leave for a "close relative".
- The norm for compassionate leave is currently three days, although some organisations prefer to leave it to the discretion of the manager.
- Many firms will consider requests for additional unpaid leave.
- All staff should be allowed time off to attend a funeral.
- A stated compassionate leave period, eg three days, should be paid time off.
- If required, counselling and other, perhaps financial, advice should be provided.
- Employers should take into account the circumstances of the bereavement, eg the death of a child, or death by a criminal or accidental act. The effect on the family should be assessed.
- Some firms provide guidance and counselling for retired staff who lose their partner.
- Some of the aspects surrounding bereavement could be preempted, such as giving staff advice on wills, pre-paid funeral plans, insurance and financial implications. This could be part of pre-retirement training.
- The death of an employee requires the employer to show the same sensitivity towards the surviving members of the person's family. There should be contact with them; a clear written statement of employment rights, pension and life assurance details and so on. The firm must be represented at the funeral and assist for as long as possible after the bereavement.

- Managers should be aware of the traumatic, sometimes devastating effect on the staff after one of their colleagues dies. Their behaviour will undoubtedly be affected and management must "coach" them through this difficult period.
- Those managers who do not perceive themselves as "social workers" should reflect on the impression the handling of these matters will have on the rest of the staff.
- For further help and information contact:
  - **Bereavement Counselling Training**
    British Association of Counselling
    Tel: 0788-78328
  - **Bereavement Support Service**
    102 Dickson Road
    Blackpool
    FY4 2BU
    Tel: 0253 402600.

CASUAL WORKERS

This place runs on casuals. And the customer doesn't know who's a casual and who isn't. Of course, they don't care as much, they're not bothered about training or standards.

These comments on the casual worker issue were made at a seminar concerned with individual responsibility for maintaining standards. The speaker of the above statements was a full-time banqueting waitress, and she spoke from the heart. Her words get to the core of the problem. How can the hospitality industry compromise the need for staffing flexibility, as personified by the "casual", and the attainment and maintenance of a quality service and product to the customer?

Each business must analyse its own variations in trading volume, its peaks and troughs and its need for sudden and considerable increases in staff numbers. Hotels with large conference and banqueting facilities may have such a need, and others near airports may experience, and delight in, the occasional delayed flight of 180 passengers needing food and accommodation overnight.

Many establishments develop groups of "regular" casuals — individuals who have the right uniform, know the procedures and standards and can be relied upon to respond to the call. Such casuals, if properly trained and motivated, may well be most valuable workers.

Legally, however, they may be considered to be developing a verbal contract and some have been able to claim unfair dismissal if the arrangement has been going on for over two years, as if they had enjoyed continuous service

However, the major test of the employment status of the casual worker is from 1983, a case following a dispute between a group of regular casuals and the Trusthouse Forte Hotel Group (now Forte Hotels).

The court found that casual workers were not "employees" with the resultant "employment rights", because:

(a) their engagement could be terminated without notice
(b) they had the right to decide whether to work or not
(c) there was no obligation to provide work
(d) casual workers were seen as independent contractors
(e) custom and practice has built up such that casuals are engaged under a "contract for service".

As with any people-situation, classification of details can prevent misunderstanding and dispute. Many firms now issue casuals with a "casual worker agreement" — a written statement of the terms and conditions under which they are engaged (not employed). The agreement should refer to the following:

(a) a casual worker is engaged, not employed
(b) a casual worker has the right to accept or refuse the offer of work
(c) full details of terms and conditions, such as the rate of pay, uniform, laundry, disciplinary procedure, taxis for late workers
(d) the importance of attending training sessions, of health, hygiene and safety
(e) the importance of following procedures and standards under supervision
(f) when the engagement first commenced, and, if the worker is then taken on full or part-time, will this period count for continuous service?
(g) casual workers should complete a tax form, P46A or B, and submit their NI number.

Whether businesses have such an agreement or merely establish a verbal arrangement, it is important to consider the effect of casual workers on the business, the customers and the full-time staff.

Proper training and supervision of casuals is essential, thus integrating them into the workforce and not just allowing them to turn up in incorrect, dirty uniforms with their service equipment in their back pockets.

COMMUNICATION

(See also: "Participation", "Staff Handbook")

Consistently clear communication is the way to "get the message across". It is vital when managing people to keep them fully in the picture on matters affecting them, to avoid unfounded fears and potentially damaging misunderstandings. Many firms fail to appreciate that their workforce is interested to know, to be involved and, above all, need to feel secure in their livelihood. Effective communication can satisfy these desires. Too often, decisions are made, changes are implemented, plans are brought forward or postponed, and some of the people directly or indirectly affected are not involved or informed.

Formula for effective communication

This "formula" should be close to hand as a reminder every single day:

question no. 1 What have I learned, decided upon or done today, that I must tell someone else?

question no. 2 Who should I tell, when, and by what method should I communicate?

Methods of communication to employees

One cannot communicate too often information which affects people's livelihoods. Methods will vary from one organisation to another, according to the size of the workforce, and the complexity and spread of business locations. The methods listed below are predominantly physical systems, but one of the most effective, cheap and quick means of communicating is to *talk* to people and to *listen* to them. Consider the methods below and review the firm's systems.

- *Noticeboards*   Attractive
  Readable
  Well positioned
  Up to date

- *Staff meetings*   Consultative
  All involved
  Planned
  "Two-way" communication

- *Terms and*   Written statement
  Conditions   Key aspects on noticeboards
  Clear amendments notified

- *Staff handbook*

- *Newsletter leaflet*

- *Company newspaper*

- *Use of flip chart* In employee restaurant
  posters   In changing rooms
  Wages office area
  Live-in areas
  Recreation areas

- *New standards*   Briefing sessions
  information   Flip chart posters in back-of-house
  areas

- *Information slip*
  in wage packet

- *Focus groups*   Three to six members of staff
  Consultative
  Discuss changes, plans
  Discuss issues affecting them and the
  customer

- *Special sessions*
  for some work
  groups

  Night staff
  Casual workers
  Part-timers
  Weekend staff

- *Daily briefing*
  meetings

  Management
  Heads of department
  Relevant staff

- *Distribution*
  checklists

  Ensures all staff informed

- *Communication*
  responsibility

  Delegated to one manager
  Each department has one employee
  responsible for information spread

COUNSELLING

(See also: "Emotions")

Counselling skills have relevance to many interpersonal situations between managers and employees, from disciplinary and grievance matters, to personal problems affecting work performance. All managers and supervisors should be made aware of the tell-tale signs in the performance, attitude and conduct of their staff which could be rectified by a counselling discussion. Indicators include:

(a) unsatisfactory conduct
(b) sudden unsatisfactory performance
(c) erratic performance
(d) irritability and rows with colleagues
(e) irritability with customers
(f) regular absences
(g) obsessions, including "workaholism".

Such behaviour may be caused by a list of reasons, some work-related, many the result of personal or domestic difficulties, and very often exacerbated by a feeling that there is nobody to help or to try to understand. Uncharacteristic outrageous behaviour can indeed be a "cry for help". Counselling — a purposeful confidential discussion — can at least provide someone to listen, and may result in a mutual plan to solve the problem.

As the person responsible for personnel issues, the human resource manager will often be the individual to whom counselling needs are referred by line management and supervisors. This will often happen when a first level discussion between employee and supervisor has been unable to address the matter satisfactorily.

When carrying out a more formal counselling session the following factors should be taken into account:

- *Obtain background information*
  From supervisor
  From personal file

- *Approach individual*
  Do not frighten off
  Informal approach: "Come for a chat"

- *Counselling location*
  Very private
  Comfortable, relaxed
  No desk barriers

- *Gain trust*
  Very private
  Assure of desire to help
  Listen

- *Get individual to talk*
  Do not dominate
  Do not take over
  Do not give own opinions
  Do not make decisions for the individual
  Be a good listener
  Ask open questions

- *Use body language*
  Head nodding
  Facial concern
  Eye contact

- *Tone of voice*
  Calm, serious
  Encourage verbally:
  "Go on", "Tell me"

- *Avoid note taking*

  Causes employee's concern
  Who will see the note?

- *Discuss optional courses*

  Best if employees work out situation for themselves
  Individuals must be committed to the course of action.

- *Agree course of action*

  What? How?
  Who involved?
  Who will be told what?
  Notes could be made now
  Make sure action happens
  Monitor progress

- *Further information*

  British Association for Counselling,
  37 Sheep Street
  Rugby
  Warwickshire
  Tel: 0788 78328

- Further reading

  Counselling, Michael Megranahan, IPM 1989

DIET

Whether we take much notice or not, all of us have become more aware of the need for "healthy living". The Government, the media, and even food retailers themselves, are constantly urging us to consider a better-balanced diet. Food packaging is now covered with dietary information. We are influenced strongly by the media through advertisements and television programme content to review our lifestyle, questioning how much alcohol we drink, how much exercise we take and what we eat. Employers cannot ignore these generally positive trends. Though diet is very much an individual consideration, employers must provide an environment at work which supports and accommodates the "healthier eater".

The benefits are clear. Healthier workers have much lower absence rates, are happier and livelier at work, and their productivity is much enhanced. Diet can be the cause of many sickness absences and lead to sluggish, ineffective performance. The hospitality business is vibrant, fast-moving, and needs employees with energy and relative fitness, and a physical and mental agility which can provide better customer service and enable them to cope more effectively with stress and pressure.

The nature of the business often makes people eat more and eat quickly. Lost energy is replaced by large amounts of carbohydrate. Meal breaks tend to be short — a fast and furious lunch followed by a quick coffee and a cigarette. Late shift workers, leaving at 11 o'clock or later, need to unwind over a drink, a smoke and possibly a Chinese takeaway. It is not a recipe for healthy living.

The hospitality business in particular should be sensitive to exerting some influence on its employees' eating habits, especially via the staff restaurant. Managers and the Head Chef must agree a variety of menus, with provision for "healthier" dishes. This formula too often results in a pathetic salad bar with food notable for its lack of excitement — almost designed to get employees running back to the chips and burgers. Consider the following points:

- The employee restaurant should serve food of variety, should influence choice and style, and should properly respond to the demand for healthy dishes, hot and cold, and the increasing number of vegetarians.
- Employees should be consulted over the menus.
- The needs of employees who have food allergies (often dairy products or red meat, for example) should be taken into account.
- The firm should organise advice and briefing sessions with employees on diet and the implications for their health, including very serious illnesses such as heart disease.
- Employees should be encouraged to attend weight-watcher classes, aerobics and sports clubs.
- The Health Education Authority (HEA) produces many useful leaflets, such as those associated with its campaign "Look After Your Heart". These can be obtained free of charge from the HEA (address in Appendix 3). The HEA will also, for large organisations, run awareness and "test your fitness" days in-house, which can be fun and influential.
- The HCIMA has produced a useful technical brief on *Implementing Healthy Catering Practice*.

DYSLEXIA

This topic, also known as "special learning difficulty", is included as it is a much misunderstood condition that is a more frequent problem than many imagine. It is common for highly intelligent people to appear to have difficulties in writing, spelling or reading, or in other areas such as dexterity, memory and numeracy. The Dyslexia Institute estimates that 10 per cent of the population may be affected by some form of dyslexia, and that four out of every 100 people will actually need special help.

Recognition

Very often, dyslexia may show up as a particular "block" in one area of work, when performance in other aspects is significantly better. The list below itemises the main symptoms which could alert management to a dyslexia problem and therefore may influence assessments of overall ability, or proposals of alternative work and procedures where the condition may be less intrusive. For example, an application form with particularly poor spelling or lacking order and accuracy may be due to dyslexia, and on interview the applicant may perform much better and have a real chance of employment. Symptoms of dyslexia include:

(a) inaccurate reading of numbers
(b) poor short-term memory
(c) confused telephone messages
(d) poor spelling
(e) difficulty in taking notes or copying
(f) confusion over the times of appointments
(g) misreading instructions
(h) poor sense of direction
(i) avoidance of written reports and memos
(j) difficulty in form-filling
(k) slow reading of letters.

Many youngsters will have dyslexia problems noticed at school but many leave education with an unidentified condition. People become increasingly conscious of deficiencies in areas such as those above and through embarrassment may go to great lengths to disguise or cover up their problem.

Though dyslexia, as a form of brain coordination disorder, cannot be cured, the Dyslexia Institute can help by advising on strategies to overcome the most unfortunate outcomes of the problem. The Job Centre may also refer an employed or unemployed individual to Assistance Towards Employment (ASSET) or the Employment Rehabilitation Centre.

Further information

The Dyslexia Institute has centres throughout the country, and details of the nearest location and other relevant literature should be obtained from the head office, at 133 Gresham Road, Staines, Middlesex, TW18 2AJ, telephone number 0784 463851.

EMOTIONS

(See also: "Counselling")

Emotion and the expression of inner feelings and attitudes will inevitably affect the behaviour of employees including their work performance, and therefore good management is needed. Whether there is a workforce of two or 200, emotions will surface and the very nature and pressure of the business will often exacerbate such feelings as anger, frustration, worry, envy and fear. In his very useful book *Improve Your People Skills*, Peter Honey poses the question of whether feelings cause behaviour or behaviour causes feelings. He is sure that feelings and behaviour do not occur in a vacuum: "something happens to trigger it".

At the heart of counselling people in an unhelpful state of some form of emotion is the need to discover the external force or trigger which has caused such feelings and ultimately affected outward behaviour. The effectiveness of the human resource manager's approach to handling emotion in an employee will determine if the issue can be resolved quickly and satisfactorily, or whether the problem continues to reduce performance and productivity as well as affect other employees detrimentally. The hotel and catering business can be susceptible to emotional difficulties, with small groups working together very closely in often hectic pursuit of targets and deadlines. A busy restaurant, a large banquet, the check-in of a tour, are all daily situations which put behavioural pressure on employees. Add to this personal problems, inter-employee conflict and inter-departmental tensions (eg kitchen/restaurant) and there is a "soup" of potential emotional expression.

The social life of employees will often be extensions of the work group, particularly in hotels with live-in staff. Employees go out together, drink and generally socialise together, and the possibility of emotional problems such as "love-life" complications, can readily spill over into the work situation.

As a result, the human resource manager may have to deal with:

(a) fears and distress
(b) temper and aggression
(c) irritability
(d) disappointment
(e) self-pity
(f) disillusionment
(g) worry and anxiety.

Assessment of the cause on an individual basis must be objective and rid of preconceived assumptions. As with counselling, it is necessary to get to the root cause and background, and then consider solutions. Tragic events such as attempted and even actual suicide, can often be followed by someone saying "I really didn't realise how serious it was". On the other hand, many emotions emanate from trivial causes and all a person needs is a jolt to get him or her to see the futility and stupidity of their behaviour.

Own behaviour

Behaviour affects behaviour, and the human resource manager's own responses or method of handling an emotional problem is the key to its solution:

- assess the background to the situation
- assess the individual's normal and previous behaviour and emotions
- get relevant information from the supervisor
- determine a satisfactory outcome to the discussion
- be controlled and positive

- do not be unduly affected by tears, they may need to come out or they may be a ploy to exert emotional blackmail
- show empathy and gain rapport, by putting oneself in the individual's shoes
- never react aggressively to temper — be firm and calm, and diffuse the aggression by a sensible, controlled example
- be prepared to be very assertive, as people may need "straightening out" and to be motivated to sort themselves out, and get on with the job
- ask many open questions to get to the basic cause of the problem
- personnel people should always invest in a large box of 3-ply tissues for these occasions.

HEALTH AND SAFETY

(See also: "Accidents", "Hygiene")

Legislation

There is much legislation which applies to health and safety. It is not the purpose here to detail such statutory obligations but to consider the practical application and the good practices that result. For more detail on relevant legislation refer to *Croner's Catering*. In particular, it is necessary to be familiar with the following:

(a) the Health and Safety at Work Act (HASAWA) 1974
(b) the Fire Precautions Act 1971
(c) the Control of Substances Hazardous to Health Regulations (COSHH) 1988
(d) the Health and Safety (First Aid) Regulations 1981
(e) the Health and Safety Information for Employees Regulations 1989.

Businesses, small and large, must take note of such legislation and continue to update themselves, as further regulations will undoubtedly follow through EC directives and UK Government policy. Many people worry about "not breaking the law", or having to comply with "idiotic rules" which may not seem practical or appropriate. The important aspect is to consider the good business sense of healthy and safe premises, environment and working systems, equipment and procedures. Injuries and poor health in employees merely lead to absence, low efficiency and productivity, and high costs in sick pay schemes and extra wages to cover absence. Furthermore, employers should not be hypnotised by minimum legal requirements, but must remember their common law duties of care and good faith towards employees.

A graphic example of the need to avoid negligence and carry out the common law duty to provide safe systems of work is the case of a metal worker who tragically lost an eye in an accident at work. The court found that the company had honoured its statutory duty to train the employee in safety procedures and to make available protective goggles. The fact that these were not worn by many workers was revealed, and the court found the company was in breach of its common law duty by not adequately supervising the work, and by not enforcing through instruction the wearing of the goggles. In other words, it is clearly ridiculous to allow employees working with molten metal not to wear protective eye-coverings. So, in all health and safety issues take note of the statutory requirements but also ensure that common sense and good practice are applied when implementing procedures. Not to do so can lead to very high compensation payments to injured workers, and may have a long-term effect on workforce productivity and morale.

When reviewing the firm's approach to health and safety, consider the practical measures noted below.

1. By specifically analysing the type and size of the business, compile a written health and safety policy, detailing the systems, procedures, training and attitudes which will ensure a healthy, safe place in which to work.
2. Identify specific hazards in the building, in departments and in the working systems.
3. Identify aspects of the business which could provide a health risk, including dangerous substances (eg cleaning materials).
4. Identify dangerous equipment (eg cutting machines or high-power electrical appliances) and detail the safety precautions in their operation.
5. Provide any relevant safety clothing, such as safety shoes, gloves and overalls.

6. Ensure that employees are given as much information as possible (required by the 1989 regulations) on all health and safety matters.

7. Appoint a senior employee as overall supervisor for health and safety.

8. Appoint an employee in each area or department as a health and safety representative who can report problems, hazards, etc to the senior person responsible.

9. Ensure there is an effective and quick reporting system, so that dangerous circumstances may be acted upon immediately.

10. Organise a systematic training programme for all employees. For example:

    Health and safety training   —   every six months
    Hazard spotting exercises   —   ongoing
    Fire training (by law)   —   every six months, or every three months for night and live-in staff.

11. Ensure that *all* such training is fully recorded and accurate by name of employee, date and training content.

12. Develop a positive relationship of liaison with the Environmental Health Officer. It is better to seek advice rather than *hope* not to receive a visit.

13. Be aware that everyone on the premises is the responsibility of the firm in matters of their health and safety: this includes customers and outside contractors. Contract caterers must act as if any person in the catering area is under their supervision, whether directly employed by them or not. *Sime v Sutcliffe Catering Scotland Ltd* (1990), was a case where an employee of the client company slipped on aspic jelly resulting in a back injury. This was considered by the court to be negligence, and as Sutcliffe Catering was in charge of the catering operation, it was found negligent.

14. Emphasise to all employees that any individual may be found negligent and prosecuted, so there is a vital personal responsibility to ensure that everyone works safely and with other employees in mind.

15. It is advisable to devise a health questionnaire for all new employees, and to ensure that all employees know that they must immediately report infectious illnesses such as those noted below:

(a) diarrhoea
(b) vomiting
(c) gastro-enteritis
(d) dysentry
(e) sceptic conditions
(f) skin infections.

Doctors' clearance notes should be obtained before they recommence work. Appendix 2 includes an example of a health questionnaire.

HYGIENE

(See also: *Croner's Catering*)

The objectives of good hygiene practice are to ensure safe food standards, to eliminate the possibility of food poisoning and to avoid allegations that the business has not shown due diligence in the pre-paration, storage and service of food. This topic is particularly important at present due to the enforcement in January 1991 of the Food Safety Act 1990. This legislation tightens the powers of Environmental Health Departments, sets new standards on food safety, and, for human resources managers to note, imposes more rigorous training needs, though not all these provisions on training have been fully enforced yet.

The main points to note are that:

(a) all food businesses must be registered with the Environmental Health Department
(b) relevant full-time catering staff need training that encompasses food temperatures including cold storage in preparation and when waiting to be served
(c) many modern refrigerators keep food at 5°C in any case
(d) it is the intention that *all* food handlers must undergo compulsory hygiene training. There is uncertainty as to the effective date of enforcement of this provision but this is likely to be in 1992.
(e) many firms are pre-empting the enforcement of food handler training by ensuring that all such staff attain basic food hygiene training, many certificated under the auspices of the Royal Society for Health (RSH) or the Royal Institute of Public Health (RIPH) or the Institute of Environmental Health Officers (IEHO)

(f) food handler hygiene training may be provided by various bodies, including the Environmental Health Department, local colleges, the Hotel and Catering Training Company, or through in-company hygiene and catering departments. The average cost for the food hygiene certificate course is £35 per person. Training should cover all relevant employees, including kitchen porters.

(g) it is necessary to keep in touch with the trade press on further clarification and the publication of a code of practice. Advice and information may also be obtained from the HCIMA via its Technical Advisory Group

(h) training of staff should be systematic, regularly "refreshed" (eg every six months) and interesting. If the firm has a hygiene training pack it should not just be handed out time after time, to the boredom of longer service employees. Updates through staff meetings should take place and noticeboard posters used.

(i) it is vital to have precise records of any training given, as these may be inspected by Environmental Health Officers (EHO) as part of their visit

(j) Environmental Health Officers may make an inspection "at any reasonable time", so food safety and personal hygiene standards must be mentioned daily as an integral part of duty management and supervision

(k) many managers have taken an open and positive appraoch to EHOs, actually contacting *them*, inviting them to advise and help. This is rather more professional than hoping they will not visit

(l) the firm may wish to ask all food handlers to sign a declaration regarding infectious illnesses: a sample pro forma is included in Appendix 2.

INDUSTRIAL RELATIONS

(See also: "Participation")

A book on matters of personnel management in many sectors of the economy would require a much greater emphasis on industrial relations, when defined as the system of regulating employment issues between employers and employees through their associations. In a great many hospitality businesses, trade union involvement is minimal.

Restaurants and hotels have union membership levels of negligible amounts, though industrial and institutional outlets may have up to 20 per cent of staff as trade union members. The nature and development of the hospitality industry has led to a low involvement with unions. There are many small firms, with transient or temporary staff, and terms and conditions agreed on an individual basis have mitigated against collective bargaining and the union ability to "organise" the workforce. In truth, many areas of the trade have seemed of very little attraction to the unions themselves, and membership recruitment campaigns have generally been half-hearted. Above all, the people who work in the hospitality industry have no background or tradition which encompasses trade union membership and are themselves quite hostile to such concepts.

Recognition of a trade union usually only occurs when more than 50 per cent of employees are members. The largest UK hotel and catering employer, Forte PLC, has recently agreed with the GMB (general workers union), that it may represent its staff at two hotels where the 50 per cent figure has been exceeded. Therefore, shop stewards may be appointed and they will be given time off work to attend union training programmes.

It can be seen that each business and each group of workers needs to be viewed separately. It is a fact that major trade unions are more interested in service sector industries, as their membership levels have plummeted due to the decline of manufacturing industry in the 1980s.

- Trade unions are likely to step up their recruitment campaigns in the hospitality industry to increase levels of membership.
- The management attitude to trade unions should be professional, working with them as partners if necessary, and not in a frightened, paranoid and hostile atmosphere.
- Bad management leads employees to seek external help and redress. Good employment practices are therefore essential.
- Employee relations are important, whether there is union involvement or not. It is vital to consult employees, listen to them and react to their problems and grievances.
- Good practice in the 1990s is undoubtedly going to lead to increased employee involvement and participation in the way businesses are run. EC directives and the Social Charter will increase pressure in this area.

- The emphasis of the recent Green Paper on industrial relations, put forward by the Conservative Government, is to preserve and develop the rights of the individual, and to see a trade union as having a much wider role than collective bargaining on pay and conditions. Advisory, welfare and health and training roles are seen as appropriate to the union of the future.

INDUSTRIAL RELEASE PLACEMENTS

The hotel and catering industry is clearly a business where theory must be backed by practical experience. Hence, most further and higher education courses in hotel and catering operations have developed periods of industrial release, normally in the middle section, and varying from three to twelve months in duration. This period of exposure to the industry is very influential on these mainly young people, and can reinforce career ambitions or, at worst, shatter illusions totally. Research completed at Brighton Polytechnic endorsed the widely held "common sense" view that a poor or unhappy experience during industrial release leads the individual either to choose another sector of the hospitality industry or to leave it altogether on completion of the degree or Higher National Diploma.

Employers and industrial tutors have produced jointly a code of practice for work experience in management courses for the hotel and catering industry. It describes the purpose of work experience as:

(a) to develop individual maturity, self-awareness and confidence
(b) to provide some structured practical experience of the industry, its operations, its customers and its staff
(c) to consolidate skills learned during studies and appreciate industrial standards and levels of performance
(d) to enable industry to demonstrate the career potential that is available.

The whole system of arranging and monitoring industrial placements is being reviewed constantly, under the auspices of the Industrial Tutors Group (ITG), a body of industrial tutors from the educational institutions offering hotel and catering management subjects. At the time of writing, the chair is Mrs Sandra Watson of Napier Polytechnic, Edinburgh. This group has particularly tackled the question of better industry liaison, overseas placements and improved preparation by students before taking on their placements. The last point is highlighted by the fact that many industrial release students have detailed learning objectives and desired outcomes from their period of training compiled in conjunction with their tutor and employing firm. This approach, often referred to as a personal learning contract, gives student and host employer a better framework in which to organise training.

Improving the quality of placements

- Foster and develop close, strong links with providing colleges and their industrial tutors.
- Agree specific arrangements with a college over how many students the firm will take, when, what training they will receive and the terms and conditions of employment.
- Be involved in the formulation of specific objectives, the personal learning contract, and do not forget the needs of the business and the pressure on supervisors and trainers.
- If possible, phase placements over the year, so that trainers do not have too many all at once.
- Interview all placement candidates in the normal way. Such practice assures the firm of a suitable "employee" and is a beneficial experience for the student.
- Keep management and supervisors fully aware of their commitment to industrial placement training. Inform them of all details regarding an individual student and the objectives and keep reminding them of an imminent new "trainee" about to join their department. Placements can often go wrong when heads of departments do not really want one.
- Monitor the student's progress as often as possible and if concerns arise, do not hesitate to contact the college's industrial tutor.
- Although placements should be structured and based on objectives, students must be fully exposed to the vitality and flexibility which is part of the challenge and excitement of the industry. It is when students are used indiscriminately to fill in for job vacancies that they get a raw deal and become disillusioned. It is probably better for a student to spend six months in one job or department and really learn and contribute, rather than to flit from one department to another, learning little and contributing nothing.

- "Talent-spot" all industrial placement students: they could well figure in longer-term succession planning, and therefore keeping in touch once they are back at college can be of mutual benefit to student and business.

INDUSTRIAL TRIBUNALS

The purpose of these "courts" is to provide a means for employees to seek redress from an employer on the grounds that the employer has breached employment legislation. The tribunal has jurisdiction to deal with the following:

(a) the Equal Pay Act 1970
(b) the Health and Safety at Work Act 1974
(c) the Sex Discrimination Act 1975
(d) the Employment Protection Acts 1975, 1980, 1982 and 1988
(e) the Employment Protection (Consolidation) Act 1978
(f) the Race Relations Act 1976
(g) the Wages Act 1986.

In effect, 75 per cent of tribunal hearings deal with claims of unfair dismissal, and only a third of these actually reach the court room. Most are withdrawn or settled out of court when one side feels that its case is a hopeless one and wishes to avoid costly and embarrassing failure at the tribunal.

The tribunal itself consists of an experienced solicitor or barrister as chairman and a representative of the Confederation of British Industry (CBI) and the Trades Union Congress (TUC). An appeal procedure is available following a decision, on a point of law only, and this is heard by the employment appeal tribunal (EAT).

The fairness of its employment policies and procedures will clearly determine how much time a firm spends in one of the 30 or so tribunal centres in the UK.

It is here that detailed records of evidence, statements and general administration of employment issues will all come under scrutiny. Many cases are lost by employers because of technical administrative inefficiencies rather than incorrect or unfair decisions.

An employee is usually referred to a tribunal by the Department of Employment, a solicitor or an organisation such as the Citizens Advice

Bureau. Once the firm is notified that an ex-employee is claiming a breach of the regulations such as unfair dismissal, it is necessary for the human resources manager to review the case with superiors and gain legal advice. Many law practices now employ a partner with specialist knowledge and experience of employment matters.

There will be a period where the firm and the solicitor or union representing the individual will correspond and attempt to settle the matter. The firm's legal advisor will swiftly assess the strength of the case and suggest going all the way to tribunal if necessary or, where significant loopholes exist, recommend a settlement out of court. It should be borne in mind that a tribunal hearing can involve the firm in very considerable expense of time, wages, travel expenses, and low productivity.

The industrial tribunal may make one of three awards if it is found that the employee was unfairly treated:

(a) re-instatement — getting the same job back
(b) re-engagement — re-employment by the firm elsewhere
(c) cash compensation.

Personal and organisational causes may mean that re-instatement and re-engagement are impractical, and indeed most awards are of cash compensation. These are normally between £2000 and £6000, but could be over £20,000 according to the individual's age, length of service, level of pay, loss of earnings and whether the firm has failed to comply with a re-instatement or re-engagement order.

LONG-SERVICE STAFF

Despite the ever-present problem of unacceptably high labour turnover in some parts of the industry, there are also many admirable examples of extraordinarily long-serving, loyal employees, some of whom may spend most of their working lives in one unit. Yet, in the battle to recruit new talent and to reduce instability, it is easy to forget the serious implications to long-service staff. We may take them for granted and fail to consider their special needs or, conversely, may put up with out-dated skills, knowledge and attitudes as they fail to move with the times. Long-service staff should be evaluated in the following ways:

(a) Have they received sufficiently sensitive training in new standards, systems and technology?

(b) Do they continue to get job satisfaction from a role they have performed for so long?

(c) Does their job need enriching and developing to motivate them sufficiently and fully utilise their experience?

(d) Have their terms and conditions kept pace, or have differentials been eroded when compared with current levels of pay commanded by more recently employed staff?

(e) Have their benefits increased with time, properly rewarding their loyalty?

(f) What is their personal situation? Do they live in, and if so what problems may there be when they do leave or retire in finding and financing a place to live?

(g) Have they had sufficient advice on finance, welfare, pensions and savings?

(h) At what point should they receive counselling on a job move for their own good? This must be very carefully handled as it is easy to give such individuals unfounded security worries.

(i) Is their performance up to standard or has their energy and motivation faded? In a world of change, this question may need to be asked and faced.

(j) Are they being taken for granted, both not enough interest being paid to their contribution and to them as people?

MOTIVATING PEOPLE

This is not an academic section on the behavioural sciences in management. Daily motivation of people at work can be a series of small and natural actions — at once simple and inexpensive. Yet, too often the following statements are heard from staff at seminars and training courses:

He doesn't even say good morning
She looks straight through you
You get no thanks for anything
Doesn't even know my name

The list below is an *aide memoire* on how to be a human being, *and* a manager.

- Always say hello or good morning or give a similar greeting
- be sincere, use eye contact
- smile at staff
- shake hands with staff
- if appropriate, a small joke will not go amiss
- use employees' names (preferably first name)
- if comfortable, get them to use your first name
- do not be over formal
- thank them and praise them, when deserved
- inform them of something pleasant, not just the unpleasant matters
- ask them how they are feeling
- ask them about family, holidays, hobbies
- keep them informed
- give them recognition
- pat them on the back — literally!
- give them incentives
- give them more responsibility
- give them copies of compliment as well as complaint letters
- involve them in decisions
- get their opinions
- get their ideas
- talk to them
- listen to them — actively and sincerely
- put their successes and achievements in writing, personally addressed and signed
- do not be afraid to discuss personal concerns
- practise MBWA (managing by wandering about)
- be a coach, not a policeman; a partner, not an "enemy of the people"
- remember birthdays and other major personal events, name spellings, nationality and background. Those with poor memories can make short notes about each of the staff as a reminder before visits. This is not cynical, but a sensible precaution by a manager committed to motivation of people.

MULTI-CULTURAL AWARENESS

There are few businesses in the hospitality industry which do not employ a workforce of multi-national origins. The industry is international in its commercial spread, its clientele and in its labour market. Britain has for many years been a place for people from all around the globe to visit for work experience, working holidays and to improve spoken English. The hotel and restaurants sector can provide these visitors with the ideal vehicle to achieve these objectives. Such movement of labour will be increased by the Single European Market, when EC nationals will have easier mobility throughout the Member States.

For people-managers — line or specialist — awareness of cultural differences is very useful in integrating teams of workers of multi-national backgrounds and getting the best out of them. Nationality and cultural background has significant influence on:

(a) behaviour
(b) attitudes
(c) characteristics
(d) values
(e) communication.

Language is clearly important when considering skill in communicating, but language is only one difference between people of different national origins. The English speaking nations give clear testament to this point: compare the cultural differences between the British, Americans, Canadians, Australians and Caribbean peoples, for example. In his book *Human Resource Management in the Hospitality Industry*, Michael Boella describes cultural awareness as "the ability to recognise and respond to cultural differences". This grasps the nettle for practical management of these issues. Recognition comes from observation and listening and interpreting. Too often we assume that other nationalities will react in the same way as ourselves. Yet cultural background may be displayed through:

(a) alternative use of words
(b) jargon
(c) colloquial expressions
(d) tone of voice
(e) directness
(f) aggression
(g) submissiveness

(h) humour

(i) body language and gesture.

Misinterpretation of any of the above can lead to a lack of understanding, confusion and conflict, and ultimately to real operational problems.

What can be done?

- Do *not* make assumptions
- question behaviour and attitudes
- find out about the cultures of the workforce
- do not use jargon
- do not use in-vogue UK expressions
- find out how overseas staff feel and what difficulties they are experiencing
- constructively "coach" overseas staff in how the behaviour of overseas employees may cause certain reactions
- team up an overseas worker with a "local", and avoid cliques of one nationality
- train or brief local staff to be aware of cultural differences
- create focus groups of mixed nationalities to discuss problems and solutions
- ensure that important instructions, eg fire precautions, are fully understood by all staff.

PARTICIPATION

(See also: "Communication", "Social Charter")

This topic covers many issues which are regularly under discussion in industrial and political circles. Sometimes participation may be referred to as employee involvement, industrial democratic management or consultation and communication.

Much will depend on the size and culture of the organisation, but few managers would deny that today some level of participation by employees is beneficial to both sides.

Forms of participation

These include:

(a) profit sharing (financial)
(b) share ownership (financial)
(c) profit or performance related pay (financial)
(d) consultation (non-financial)
(e) involvement in decisions (non-financial)
(f) informational issues (non-financial)
(g) works councils and boards (statutory).

The government and employers' associations in this country are firmly opposed to statutory participation, which is common in some European nations (eg Germany). The Social Charter further stresses the need for more worker participation and involvement, but UK feeling is usually characterised by the need for a voluntary approach.

Each business must be considered independently, but management should review employment policies and benefits to see whether employee commitment and motivation could be improved through some programme of increased participation.

Consultation through regular staff meetings could be an initial response, but gradually it may be necessary to consider more substantive and financial involvement.

REDUNDANCY

The hospitality industry, in particular hotels and restaurants, has mainly been preoccupied with recruitment and retention in the past. In 1990 and 1991 recession brought redundancies, and the outlook for 1992 is no brighter.

The recession has had serious consequences for business volume and international tourism has also been hit by terrorism and, in early 1991, by the Gulf War. Between September 1990 and March 1991, 100,000 redundancies were effected in the United Kingdom hotel and catering industry (DOE figures) — around 10 per cent of the workforce. No matter how justified staff cuts are in order to protect the business and ensure the survival of many more jobs, each case is a traumatic personal experience. Due to the history of the industry, many managers were faced with making workers redundant for the first time. There were no procedures, policies and experience. As a result there have been many regrettable stories of badly handled redundancy procedure, tarnishing the image and public relations of the business, and perhaps ensuring that large numbers of talented individuals will never return when business volumes increase in the post-recession period. The points below spell out good practical procedures which must be adopted.

Explore the alternatives

Can redundancy be avoided? It is necessary to be clear that the job, not the person, is no longer required in its current form; in addition, the following alternatives to losing a good employee should be considered:

(a) an offer of "suitable alternative employment", based on similar pay, hours of work, location and status could be made. The offer must be put in writing before the notice period has expired and the work must start immediately afterwards or within four weeks; there is a statutory right to allow a four week trial period. If either side decides the trial is unsuccessful, the employee retains the right to any redundancy payment. Payment could be lost if an employee unreasonably refuses an offer of alternative employment. Relocation involving major domestic upheaval has been considered reasonable grounds for refusal

(b) staff could be put on short-time working or on temporary lay-off, for which redundancy compensation is possible (see below)

(c) changing the terms and conditions of employment is possible but requires close examination of the original contract, and full mutual agreement between employer and employee

(d) there have been instances where staff have foregone a wage review or increase when times are hard, but good staff relations are essential for this to be possible. Management must set an example if this is considered and apply the same rules to themselves.

(e) early retirement may be another alternative, but could be costly.

Redundancy payments

- Employees qualify for redundancy pay when they have two years' service over the age of 18 and work 16 hours or more per week, or work 8 hours or more per week and have five years' service. This applies strictly to employees; casuals are not covered, for example.
  Payments are calculated as follows:
  for each year of service between ages 18-21 : half week's pay
  for each year of service between ages 21-40 : one week's pay
  for each year of service age 41 or over   : one and a half
  week's pay.
- The limits to statutory redundancy payment were last revised with effect from April 1991:
  maximum week's pay: £198
  maximum payment: £5,940
  for short time working, a day's pay: £13.65
  five days in a three month period: £68.25.
- Statutory redundancy payments are not taxable but the employer can set such sums against business expenses.
- Employers are free to exceed the statutory levels, particularly following negotiations through an independent, recognised trade union.
- If an employer is unable to pay the amount, the Department of Employment can pay from the Redundancy Fund, agreeing pay-back arrangements with the employer.
- Refusal to pay the statutory redundancy amount would lead to a claim of unfair dismissal.

Redundancy selection

- The process by which those employees who are to be made compulsorily redundant are selected must be fair, be seen to be fair and understood by all involved.
- Subjective, biased selection must be avoided and invariably causes unfair dismissal claims.
- "Last in, first out" has been a well-used system but disregards the need for a well-balanced organisation. The trend is towards objective selection based on the needs of the business. Any trade

union agreement on redundancy procedures must be observed during the selection process.
- The selective approach should involve two questions:
  Who should be made redundant?
  Why?

Communication

- Communication with those employees affected must be clear, detailed and handled with the utmost integrity and sensitivity. Verbal details should always be followed by written confirmation.
- The whole organisation must be kept informed about the process and the need for such serious steps to be taken.
- Each individual should be dealt with on a person by person basis, whether compulsory or voluntary redundancy is involved.
- Employers may wish to consider external communication, depending on the numbers affected. ACAS and the media, as well as the Department of Employment (where more than ten workers are made redundant) and the Department of Social Security could be involved.
- The human resource manager should put himself or herself in the position of those whose livelihoods are in jeopardy. They want to know, to know quickly and to be kept in the picture regularly and constantly.
- The firm may wish to set up special "quick-access" systems if large numbers of redundancies are involved, with special in-house counsellors for people to consult regarding information, and to seek advice and encouragement.

Consultation

- Consultation is the key to a fair and proper redundancy procedure. Industrial tribunals will find dismissal by redundancy unfair if there was inadequate consultation with the employee.
- There is a statutory requirement to consult fully with a recognised, independent trade union (s.99 of the Employment Protection Act 1975). This should happen at the earliest possible opportunity. The Department of Employment must be notified (whether the firm is in a trade union situation or not) (Form HR1).

- As much warning as possible must be given to an employee, stressing that the reasons for redundancy relate to the business and are not ability-related.
- The initial discussion with an individual must detail the overall situation and should be sensitive and compassionate. The individual should then be given a couple of days to consider his or her position, eg whether he or she is prepared to do other work or relocate.
- A second individual consultation should be more concerned with detail. Many personal files do not state everything about employees, so it is necessary to ascertain the extent of their prior experience, their range of skills, and their personal and family situation.

   Will they do different work? Will they move? What career counselling advice would help?
- At this stage, the employer should give full details of termination of employment by redundancy if no alternative option is found. This information should include:
   — employment rights
   — financial details
   — benefits situation
   — entitlements situation
   — pension information
   — state benefit entitlements
   — counselling and advisory services
   — job hunting help, curriculum vitae, etc.
   — interview advice and help
   — external help available such as the Job Centre, DSS, employment agencies and, for executives, outplacement agencies
   — statutory right to time off to look for a new job and to attend interviews.
- This process of help and fairness is essential if unfair dismissal claims and poor public relations are to be avoided. The days of "clear your desk by lunchtime" or "you're finished at the end of the shift" should be gone. Some recent reports suggest this is not always the case.
- Remember that dismissal through redundancy may be unfair due to:
   — failure to consult
   — unfair selection

— breach of an agreed procedure
— breach of a statutory right
— reasons connected with trade union activity
— discrimination on grounds of sex or race
— the fact that there was no genuine redundancy — it was merely used as an excuse "to get rid of" someone.

Footnote on flexibility

One of the reasons for a sudden and large number of redundancies in the hotel and catering sector is the inherent lack of flexibility within large sections of the labour force. Stereotype skills emerge too often, with little inter-departmental technical ability in evidence. Businesses should train staff to be able to work in more than one department and to develop skills in more than one area, so that when business volumes become erratic there is a valuable depth of competence in the staff.

ROTAS

Nothing causes more ill-feeling than the grievance of an employee who believes that a rota is unjust. Typical responses are as follows:

I always get the worst shifts.
He puts me on the busiest nights.
You can't plan anything in your social life!
Why couldn't we have more warning?

The compilation of an efficient and fair rota or roster is not easy, as every supervisor or manager will testify. It must be fair to the business, the customer and the employees, including management. There is no model or gold-plated system, as rotas must be tailor-made to the operation, its trading pattern and characteristics, and fully take into account the individuals involved, their capabilities and levels of co-operation. However there are a number of factors to consider.

(a) The rota must reflect the forecast business volume, ensuring correct coverage of staff to maintain a quality customer product and service. This requires an assessment of the numbers of employees required and their level of ability.

(b) Rotas must therefore be flexible, not set in the stone of tradition, and whoever is compiling them must have all relevant sales forecast information to enable proper planning.

(c) Some situations of constant levels of business, for example a contract catering unit, may lend themselves to a more fixed and recurring rota, which may help people to plan non-work activities.

(d) Rotas should be compiled as far ahead as practically possible, depending on trading patterns and business characteristics. Employees should be given the opportunity to make special requests such as for specific days off, before the rota is finally distributed.

(e) The individual responsible for the rota must do everything possible to accommodate special requests, but if it is impossible to do so an explanation should be given and some attempt made to achieve a mutual compromise.

(f) Employees must know where they can find and consult the rota in the supervisor's absence. Misunderstandings lead to staff not turning up when they should and, of course, the reverse. Either situation can lead to a reduction in customer quality and to costly low productivity.

(g) Employees benefit from their two days off together to ensure an effective rest period and split shifts should be avoided, if possible.

(h) The shift "team" should be a balanced and effective grouping, with regard to skills, experience and personality. For example, less experienced employees should not always be put on easy shifts — they improve by being on a busy shift, accompanied by highly trained colleagues.

SEXUAL HARASSMENT

This is an increasingly significant issue which should not be lightly dismissed by the hospitality industry. The European Commission code of conduct speaks of "the protection of the dignity of women and men at work". It is important to realise that any discussion of sexual harassment at work refers to both men and women. Mostly, however, harassment is by men of women and the Equal Opportunities Commission (EOC) is heavily involved in ensuring that women have equal opportunity and are encouraged to enter traditionally male-dominated jobs.

Recently, the EOC backed a former female employee of the London Borough of Islington who had been an apprentice in the buildings department. The case ended up as a claim of sexual harassment as a form of sex discrimination. It was found that the young lady had been subjected to "sexual remarks and behaviour, unwelcome physical contact, comments about what she wore, insinuation about her ability to carry out the job and poor on-site facilities". There was an out of court settlement of £15,000 — not a sum to be dismissed lightly.

Staff should realise what constitutes harassment, and in particular in departments such as the male-dominated kitchen or the female-dominated housekeeping area.

Many cases are not reported because very often the harassment is of a subordinate by a superior. It is a cynical form of asserting dominance and power over someone, and will lead to a poor working atmosphere and eventually to conflict and a reduction in efficiency.

Many companies are now formulating policies and procedures concerned with sexual harassment. ICI describes harassment as "unwanted conduct with sexual connotations whether physical or verbal, which is offensive to the recipient. It may be a single example of grossly offensive behaviour, or repeated more minor examples of such behaviour". It also states that such behaviour should be reported to the employee's immediate superior or to the personnel department, that allegations will be fully investigated with impartial confidentiality, and that any breach of the policy could lead to disciplinary action.

Smaller businesses will be unlikely to be so formal in their approach, but employers must keep in close touch with staff, listen to the everyday discussions of work groups and ensure that there is real dignity for men and women at work.

SICKNESS

(See also: *Croner's Catering*, section 4)

Since the introduction of the legal right of employees to receive statutory sick pay (SSP) in 1982, many firms have to inform their staff of the benefits due to them under both SSP and the company's sick pay scheme. Employees who are absent from work due to sickness or injury may be entitled to either or both of these sickness benefits. Most enlightened employers specify conditions of employment, and are therefore contractually bound to such arrangements. SSP payments are recovered from National Insurance contributions quite separately.

The following extract provides an example of the information to be clarified within an employment contract.

Example

Sickness Schemes and Procedures

Company scheme

You are entitled to receive sickness benefit based on the format detailed below. Benefit applies to any one calendar year, providing the specified procedures listed below are followed.

Length of service	Sickness benefit
Under 3 months	Nil
3 months - 2 years	8 weeks
2 years - 4 years	12 weeks
4 years and over	14 weeks

Company scheme procedures

1. If absent through sickness or injury, you, or someone on your behalf, must inform your superior by telephone before your rostered starting time, stating that you are unfit for work due to illness.
2. Absences of up to, and including, seven days are covered by the company self-certification process. Beyond seven days, a medical certificate is required.
3. On your return to work, you must complete a self-certification form. You will then be informed of your eligibility for payment of sickness benefit.
4. Failure to notify your superior, providing an unsatisfactory reason for absence, and/or repeated short-term absences will be treated as misconduct. False statements on the self-

certification form will also be treated as misconduct, and if payments are made on the basis of false statements, then this will be treated as gross misconduct.

5. When a longer-term illness has occurred, requiring a medical (doctor's) certificate, you must not return to duty until you have received medical certification stating that you are fit to return.

Statutory Sick Pay (SSP)

1. If you were given a Form SSP1(L) by your previous employer, you must hand this to your supervisor (or personnel department).
2. Where you only receive SSP, the rate will be in accordance with the current scales and regulations.
3. For the purposes of calculating SSP, the working week is Monday to Friday.
4. Where you receive both SSP and company benefit, the total will not exceed your normal basic wage.
5. If your SSP entitlement is exceeded (28 weeks) but you still qualify for company benefit, you will be asked to declare the amount received from the DSS, and this will be deducted from your wage. (Employer must complete Form SSP1 for employee.)
6. The rules relating to SSP are available from the DSS.
7. A PIW (period of incapacity for work) is defined as any period of four or more consecutive days, including rest days. Where PIWs are separated by not more than eight weeks, they are considered as one period, this is known as "linking".
8. The qualifying period for SSP is three days ("waiting days"). There are no waiting days for a second PIW, if linked and of four days absence or more.

The information above regarding SSP shows the need for accurate records and administration concerning all sickness absence, especially:

(a) dates of absences
(b) dates of medical certificates received

(c) days for which SSP is paid and the sums involved
(d) dates for which SSP is not paid and the reasons
(e) completion of form SSP1
(f) completion of form SSP1(L) for leavers
(g) completion of tax forms for receiving SSP payments.

Long-term Sickness

For small firms in particular, the prolonged absence of an employee through sickness, however unfortunate for the individual, may have a serious effect on the success of the business. Similarly, where an employee is absent for shorter regular periods, it is a situation which cannot be ignored. Ultimately, it comes down to a decision between keeping the job open for the individual and dismissal. The following procedure should be followed:

(a) take into full consideration the status, capability and length of service of the individual
(b) consider any opportunities for alternative employment within the organisation
(c) obtain a full and independent medical report, establishing if and when the employee could return to full duties. Contact the GP via the employee and with the latter's consent
(d) keep in close contact with the employee and meet to discuss the future, when possible
(e) ensure sickness scheme procedures are properly followed
(f) give plenty of warning on action to be taken, especially such a step as dismissal.

SMOKING

The debate over smoking at the workplace is raging throughout all industries. As the number of smokers has declined substantially in the last few years, the power of the non-smokers' lobby has increased, and firms are now responding to the implications upon smoking areas at work. The Institute of Personnel Management has shown that in 1982 only six per cent of companies had any clear, written smoking policy, but that by 1989 this figure had risen to 20 per cent, and that 80 per cent of companies had no-smoking sections. A further strong push to this trend has been the medical evidence that passive smoking (inhaling other people's tobacco smoke) can increase the risk of lung cancer in non-smokers. Employers should be aware that smokers could be at risk of lung cancer, heart disease and bronchitis as a result of their actions (or lack of action).

The Royal College of Physicians has estimated that 50 million working days are lost every year through smoking-related illness, and bronchitis even beats back-ache as the cause of more absence through sickness than any other complaint. So smoking can increase absenteeism, decrease productivity and be a heavy cost on sick pay schemes and SSP administration.

The food industries already impose restrictions on smoking in "banned" areas such as kitchens and behind bars and it will therefore often be an example of gross misconduct. However, generally a sensible approach is required, with consultation of employees and an attempt to accommodate the needs of smokers and non-smokers.

A working party could be set up, perhaps of smokers and non-smokers, to canvass opinion and make recommendations. The result may be a policy which is satisfactory to both sides and is therefore far better than a unilateral decision which would cause resentment and dissatisfaction.

Points to consider

- Designate particular areas as smoking/non-smoking
- demarcate non-smoking areas in the canteen
- allow smoking only in the recreation room
- instruct that there should be no smoking in enclosed areas, eg offices
- each work area should decide its own policy
- no-smoking rules must apply to all employees at all levels
- decide whether passive smoking is a breach of the Health and Safety at Work Act
- the lack of a designated area for smokers will cause the outside back of the hotel, or some similar spot, to become the "smoking room"
- provide educational or counselling sessions for staff who are unable to give up smoking
- any agreed policies must be communicated, explained and fully understood.

Further information

ASH (Action on Smoking and Health)
5-11 Mortimer Street
London W1N 7RH
Telephone: 071-637 9843

Health Education Authority
Hamilton House
Mabledon Place
London WC1H 9TX
Telephone: 071-631 0930

Institute of Personnel Management
IPM House
Camp Road
Wimbledon
Telephone: 081-946 9100
IPM guide: *Smoking Policies at Work* (free)

STAFF CARE

(See also: "Benefits")

Staff care is a phrase which may be used to embrace all aspects of looking after employees. It is much more than the common law "duty of care"; it is about treating staff with consideration and ensuring their dignity, whether with regard to their changing room, toilets, or the food provided in the employee restaurant.

There has been an inexcusable contradiction in many areas of the hospitality industry between superbly designed and presented guest areas, and degrading and humiliating staff areas. Responsible employers have been putting this right, aware that behaviour towards staff will in turn affect employees' behaviour towards customers.

If firms treat their staff with disdain, it is a clear signal that they do not value them as key contributors to the business and intend merely to use them in the furtherance of business objectives.

With these comments in mind, the staff areas should be inspected:

182

- Who is responsible for the staff areas?
- How are problems reported?
- Do the staff themselves care enough?
- Are there specific cleaning schedules?
- Who checks these areas on a regular basis?
- Do management visit, check and eat in the employee restaurant?
- Does the catering manager realise that the employee restaurant is another outlet for which he or she is responsible?
- Are staff consulted about these issues?
- Are there clear rules and regulations on employee behaviour?

The extent and sophistication of staff care facilities and organisation must be in line with the size of the operation but should be reviewed whether they are for three or three hundred people.

Observation will reveal much about cleanliness, the condition of fixtures and fittings, the state of the decor, and the overall ambience. The following checklist covers a range of staff care factors which may be included in a review of existing arrangements and standards:

(a) employee entrance
(b) back of house corridors
(c) changing rooms
(d) locker provision
(e) toilets
(f) shower/washing facilities
(g) employee restaurant
(h) the food and refreshments provided
(i) recreation area if provided
(j) accommodation if provided
(k) all other facilities for live-in staff
(l) taxi arrangements for early or late shifts
(m) uniform and laundering
(n) information and noticeboards
(o) the personnel and wages area
(p) night staff arrangements where applicable.

In establishments providing live-in accommodation, employers must respond to the axiom that this area is an employee's home; review the following:

(a) cleanliness, decor, fixtures and fittings
(b) size of bedroom
(c) clothes and storage space
(d) lighting, mirrors
(e) toilet facilities
(f) any cooking area
(g) lounge, television room
(h) clear rules on behaviour
(i) safety precautions
(j) responsibility for the area
(k) security arrangements
(l) special measures if accommodation is on-premises or off-premises.

Other aspects of staff care which may be appropriate to consider, include:

(a) access to health care
(b) advice and counselling arrangements
(c) hairdressing and manicure sessions
(d) make-up, general appearance help
(e) chiropody
(f) provision of shoes, hosiery
(g) sports and social events
(h) employee outings, visits
(i) vending facilities, eg for night staff.

There is clear evidence that if people are given bad living conditions, they will behave poorly. Recent reports and subsequent action in prisons confirms that human beings do react positively to better surroundings in most cases. However, it is naive to expect a wide variety and mix of people to respond in a consistent fashion. Better staff care and facilities must be accompanied by firm rules and regulations on behaviour. The consequences of anti-social conduct or wanton disregard for such facilities must be spelt out and enforced rigorously.

Management shifts must include proper inspections of all these areas, and managers should take the opportunity to talk to employees and continue the necessary process of communication and consultation on matters which affect them.

STRESS

Every day in a service sector business brings with it many in-built stress factors. A full restaurant with customers waiting for tables, an overbooked hotel, staff shortages, time pressures and deadlines, not enough business, and personal conflict are all common types of situation which create physical and mental stress which *can* enable people to perform beyond normal levels, and forces them to draw on energy supplies to overcome such challenges. Such stress can in this way be helpful and necessary. However, if stress levels are constant and prolonged, then the effects can be very harmful.

Physical symptoms such as rapid heartbeat, high blood pressure, palpitations and sweating can lead to serious illness which is sometimes fatal. The mental effects of harmful stress can lead to depression and lack of personal confidence. Often this leads individuals to attempt to reduce the stress by "artificial" means, such as heavy smoking, an increase in alcohol consumption, or even drugs.

Stress of a harmful nature is often work-based, sometimes reflecting personal and domestic difficulties. Whatever the cause, the effect on an employee is to reduce efficiency and productivity significantly, and induce regular, if short, periods of absence. Work relationships will suffer and the performance of the entire business or department may therefore be affected. Successful people managers should be on the look out for signs of stress in their employees, in their organisation and in themselves. In particular they should be aware of sudden changes in behaviour, in interpersonal relationships and in cooperation between people and teams. Irrational actions, absenteeism, and increases in smoking and drinking habits are all possible symptoms.

Sickness levels must be monitored as there is clear medical evidence that stress causes an increase in hormones which decreases the immunity to infection. Excessive absences through colds, flu and stomach complaints could actually be the result of stress. Gastric illnesses can often be a symptom of stress.

Stress factors in hospitality

- Unreasonable, uncaring management
- Service pressures
- constant interpersonal contact
- time constraints and deadlines

- physical demands
- personality and other mental demands
- inter-departmental dependancy
- lack of training or over-promotion
- embarrassment in front of people
- social and family pressures.

Stress management

- Individuals should be counselled for root causes
- management should review work methods
- review of terms and conditions of employment
- brief employees on harmful stress
- management should influence staff, and motivate themselves if necessary:
  - to reduce smoking
  - to reduce alcohol consumption
  - to eat a balanced diet
  - to take more exercise
- people should be encouraged to discuss their problems, not "bottle" them up
- various stress management techniques should be considered:
  - deep breathing exercises
  - relaxation techniques
  - "visioning" mind exercises
  - yoga
  - meditation
  - external interests and pastimes
- further information on stress management techniques may be obtained from the Health Education Council (address and telephone number in Appendix 3).

WOMEN

(See also: "Maternity Procedure", "Labour Market")

The managers of businesses, small and large, must be aware of the current and future significance of that section of the workforce made up by women. Employers must address the issue of how they can assist the female population to participate fully in the labour market. The facts are clear and influential:

(a) women currently comprise 43 per cent of the total UK workforce; often the proportion is higher in some sectors of the hospitality industry

(b) due to birth rates, and work trends population changes (demographics), women will comprise 50 per cent of the workforce by the year 2000

(c) by 2000, the current UK workforce will be larger by one million people, but women will account for 90 per cent of that increase

(d) the two age groups in which the female contingent will particularly grow, is 25-34 years and 45-54 years

(e) a 1988 survey by the CBI (Confederation of British Industry) found that 800,000 women said that they *would* return to work, but for family and domestic commitments

(f) many employers, driven by market forces to attract and retain its female workers, are improving their maternity procedures and childcare facilities to give them a competitive edge over rival companies and industries.

The hospitality and tourism industries have long drawn on the talents and services of many female workers — many sectors and workplaces being dominated by them. In many cases this was a function of the type of work (eg housekeeping, waitresses) or the influence of stereotype sector profiles, such as receptionists or personnel managers. Women are therefore of crucial importance to the hospitality business, which in turn has a great deal to offer them in terms of job and career opportunities, as well as part-time and casual work. Yet the business is now in an ever-competitive recruitment and retention scenario, where all industries are striving to attract a larger proportion of the growing female labour market. Thus employers are having to review specifically how they make special provision for the needs of female staff.

- Does the firm give any special consideration to this subject?
- What more could it do?
- What would make a woman returning to work after family commitments work for *your* firm?

A number of factors will influence this situation, from maternity procedures to unique benefits, terms and conditions of employment, and special staff care approaches and facilities. Many of these have already been covered in earlier sections of this book. Other specific points to note are:

(a) The Equal Opportunities Commission (EOC) is planning to strengthen the Equal Pay Act, and make it easier to bring an equal pay claim. Social Charter proposals, through the EC will further endorse such action and press for increased rights for part-time and temporary employees.

(b) In November 1990 the Court of Appeal gave women the right to retire at the same age as men, eg 60 or 65 — the company's normal retirement age. Forcing women to retire at 60 when a man could wait another five years was seen as an example of sex discrimination.

(c) An industrial tribunal recently pronounced that a woman who was overlooked for promotion because she was pregnant, *should* be promoted, as she had longer service and better qualifications than other candidates. The tribunal considered that there had been clear discrimination, awarded £3000 compensation and ordered that the woman must be promoted within one year of the decision.

(d) A recent survey by the Policy Studies Institute confirmed that more women are returning to work after having a baby, mostly within nine months of the birth. Many of the women expressed the view that there were still few childcare and other benefits available to encourage mothers to return to work.

(e) The main demand of "women returners" is clearly childcare — mainly workplace arrangements. Women also want more job-share and career-break schemes. The Government is lending its support and the Children Act, enforced in October 1991, will insist that local authorities review their childcare provision.

(f) Employers and other interested parties are developing a range of responses to the childcare question. Many workplace nurseries or creches have been set up, but mainly by large organisations with the ability to resource the considerable capital outlay (it is estimated that 40-50 places will cost in excess of £180,000). Less costly are childminding networks, involving local, qualified minders, providing a flexible, more simple benefit. Some local authorities provide such facilities and are also open to forms of partnership arrangement with local employers. Human resource managers should discover the situation in their own area.

(g) Further details may also be obtained from the Working Mothers Association (address in Appendix 3).

(h) Employers must also show sensitivity towards the illnesses unique to women employees. Problems associated with the menstrual cycle are too often the butt of jokes and cynicism — the result of ignorance.

For example, doctors are keen to point out that pre-menstrual syndrome is a real and often debilitating condition. Up to 40 per cent of women are affected, and the results can often be tension, irritability, fatigue, clumsiness, depression and generally being "difficult to work with". Firms with a high proportion of female workers should realise that understanding and care are necessary, with help and advice when required.

More information on this subject can be obtained from the National Association of Pre-menstrual Syndrome (address in Appendix 3).

Part 4
EXTERNAL RELATIONS

ACAS

The Advisory, Conciliation and Arbitration Service (ACAS) was set up after the 1975 Employment Protection Act with the aim of being an independent advisor to firms on their understanding of employment legislation. There had been a sudden explosion of law in the 1970s, beginning with the 1971 Industrial Relations Act, which first gave legal rights to employees if they felt they had been "unfairly dismissed".

ACAS has established itself as a vital "third party" in disputes varying from national trade union strikes, to disagreements between employer and employee.

ACAS has earned respect from employers and trade unions for its responsibility in dealing effectively with arbitration cases, and it has also produced much useful literature on employee relations to back up its free advice service.

The purpose of ACAS

- To give free, confidential advice on good employee relations practices.
- To give independent recommendations but with no legal powers to enforce.
- To produce codes of practice on employee relations (obtainable free, and often referred to in industrial tribunal cases).
- To arbitrate in major industrial disputes.
- To conciliate in local conflicts between an individual and an employer. In this way ACAS seeks to avoid the dispute going to industrial tribunal, and up to 40 per cent of such cases are settled before going to court. The usual issues are unfair dismissal claims or a claim of discrimination such as on the grounds of race or sex.
- To provide an independent service to employer and employee when they are parting company "amicably", in order to ensure

that any severance pay, terms and conditions are fair and equitable. This free service smooths the way forward and prevents further recourse to an industrial tribunal.

This is discussed in more detail shortly.

ACAS: how to use it

Primarily, ACAS should be used as a source of advice and help. By direct contact or through reference to its many booklets and codes of practice, ACAS provides employers, with a wealth of experience and knowledge. The regional offices are staffed by conciliation officers and advisors who are experienced practitioners in the field of employee relations. Advice can be sought on issues such as:

(a) personnel records
(b) employee problems
(c) analysis and statistics
(d) staff relations and communication
(e) disciplinary procedures
(f) grievance procedures
(g) trade union activities
(h) change of owning company
(i) job evaluation.

ACAS can be invaluable in helping to settle complicated personal disputes between the employer and a member of staff, often of long service. It is always better for both parties in such cases to avoid a long drawn-out case which ends up at an industrial tribunal, possibly drags on to an employment appeal tribunal and certainly ends in acrimony.

With rapid changes in organisational structure, technology and skills required, there comes a time when a firm and an individual may have to part company. It may not be a simple case of redundancy and there could be disagreement and misunderstanding.

Any regional centre of ACAS will put firms in touch with one of its highly experienced conciliation officers. The case can be discussed over the phone or arrangements can be made to meet the conciliation officer, normally at the place of work.

ACAS will be keen to check that the firm has spoken at length with the employee concerned and has gone a long way towards obtaining agreement with the individual. This will often cover a detailed financial settlement encompassing matters such as the notice period, payment in lieu, entitlement, compensation, or an ex-gratia payment (tax free) granted by the company in respect of seniority and long service.

The process concludes on a day when the employer, the employee and the conciliation officer meet, both separately and together, to ratify the agreement, and very often to finalise the details of termination of employment.

The firm should have prepared in advance items such as:

(a) two private meeting rooms
(b) letter clarifying *all* the details of the agreement
(c) a cheque covering the financial settlement
(d) details on pension rights
(e) any other details concerning contractual rights
(f) an itemised pay statement
(g) P45 tax form.

The procedure is normally as follows. The firm meets the conciliation officer first, confirming in detail the agreement reached or to be reached, and the events leading up to this. Where appropriate, the financial settlement should be explained fully with all the relevant documents available. The conciliation officer is *not* just a "rubber stamp", and is there in a totally independent capacity to see that fairness and reasonableness are attained. Most officers will make notes at this stage but very little comment or opinion will be forthcoming.

Next the conciliation officer will have a private meeting with the employee, discussing the situation in detail and ensuring that the employee's side is fully heard. Following this process, the officer will return to the firm's representatives and review the content of the discussion with the employee. Often some small issues will have arisen which need clarification. On occasion, an unexpected problem will spoil the deliberation, perhaps postponing the conclusion of the event. However, if the agreement has been well prepared, the conciliation officer will write out a Form COT-3, which summarises the main facts of the settlement.

This conciliation process binds both parties. Neither the employee nor the applicant can take the matter any further, which is particularly important where recourse to an industrial tribunal is still a possibility. The Form COT-3, describes the agreement as being in full and final settlement, and is signed by the firm's representative and the employee. Each party has a copy, and at this point any cheque, termination details and documents may be handed to the employee. The firm may wish to confirm that it would be prepared to respond to any request for references from potential future employers.

Contacting ACAS

The ACAS head office is in London and all telephone numbers of the undernoted regional offices are in Appendix 3.

ACAS Regional Offices are in London, Birmingham, Bristol, Cardiff, Fleet, Glasgow, Leeds, Manchester and Newcastle-upon-Tyne.

BRITISH HOSPITALITY ASSOCIATION

Formerly the British Hotel Restaurants and Caterers Association, this organisation is to be relaunched under its new name in early 1992. The change to British Hospitality Association (BHA) further endorses the view that the various sectors of the industry need to have a single identity within the economy and society. The aims of this relaunch are:

(a) to provide a strong voice for the industry as its trade association
(b) to ensure that the views of the industry are heard
(c) to ensure that the full role of hospitality in the economy is understood
(d) for the organisation to become as well known as, for example, the National Farmers' Union
(e) to represent the industry in discussions and dealings with external bodies, in particular the government.

The Association is supported by the leading employers in this country, many of whom participate in its activities. There is a range of advisory panels, addressing key issues of the day and publishing reports, advisory information and statistics. Much of the Association's recent efforts have been concerned with:

(a) the implications of the Food Safety Act
(b) food hygiene regulations
(c) metrication of measures and sale of wine by the glass
(d) the development of contract catering.

There are advisory panels covering restaurants and catering, hotels, contract catering, motorway service areas, career development and employment and external relations.

The Career Development and Employment Committee, which steers the human resource management area, is of particular note to hotel and catering firms. Member organisations may gain excellent help and advice from this office on a whole range of employment matters, in particular terms and conditions and overseas industrial placements and transfers. The address and telephone number is provided in Appendix 3.

CITIZENS ADVICE BUREAU

Towns and cities throughout the country provide their populations with the services of a Citizens Advice Bureau. These bureaux, normally staffed by part-time experts, can differ greatly in the extent of the services they provide, as they are fundamentally independent and develop to suit their particular community. Enquiries are dealt with by phone, letter or personal visit.

The members of the bureau will be trained and briefed to give general advice and to use the national information systems network. Often, though, they specialise in the following areas:

(a) employment matters
(b) Department of Social Security issues
(c) personal finance matters
(d) business finance issues.

Depending on the expertise of the particular bureau, the individual enquirer may be helped directly, or referred to a specific source of assistance and advice. In case of wrong advice being given, the bureau employees are insured against detrimental consequences.

Contact with a Citizens Advice Bureau by the human resource manager will clearly be in the area of employment, including the resolution of personal problems. Some bureaux, where there are very specific skills, will actually follow through an employment issue. Indeed, some unfair dismissal and other employment disputes have prompted a bureau to represent the individual right through to the industrial tribunal.

COLLABORATION

(See also: "Competitors")

In many areas of today's society, we are seeing moves towards collaboration, rather than isolationism and confrontation. In business, there has been a marked shift from predatory takeover, to mutually agreed merger and joint venture. In politics, notably within the EC, nations are more readily entering into collaborative projects, seeing the benefits of cooperation and joint interests.

The hospitality industry is not immune to such trends. While remaining competitive and success-oriented, there is a move from hard-nosed independence to a realisation that by working together there may be far greater success for a greater number of firms and individuals.

Even within larger organisations, departments and divisions are helping each other rather than trying to win points, or win some meaningless and costly game of internal politics. Smaller firms will especially gain from establishing healthier links with competitors and other external organisations. It is a means of pooling resources and getting a better return on those resources; it combines strengths, reduces weaknesses and can open up opportunities which a small business could not exploit on its own.

Clearly, individual success and improvement are the objectives of each firm, and collaboration can provide a cost-effective means to achieve success, as well as involving a healthier business environment.

Example of "Piggy-back" Training schemes

Training is a problem for many of those operating a smaller hospitality outlet. Small numbers of employees may mean that organising training is difficult: there may not be the necessary skill in-house and engaging an external training consultant may be very costly. Collaboration with other local hotel and catering firms could help. Costs could be shared, places on each other's courses could be made available, and the whole experience could benefit employees and improve performance standards in a cost-effective manner.

The term "Piggy-back" Training has been styled by the Training and Enterprise Council (TEC) in Oldham, and offers small firms a real opportunity to provide excellent training programmes in the way that a large organisation could resource internally.

Other forms of collaboration

- A joint recruitment campaign with local firms.
- Sharing live-in accommodation facilities.
- Producing general literature on employment matters, perhaps a leaflet for Job Centres.
- Collaboration with all relevant organisations, proactively forging mutually beneficial relationships, including Job Centre, HCIMA, BHA, TECs.
- Collaboration with local colleges and schools, constantly improving industry and education links. Sometimes known as "Compacts", these ventures really can assist longer-term recruitment and training issues.
- Collaboration with local government on employment matters, many towns having a forum of employers and other interested parties which can address local and very specific problems affecting a business.

COLLEGES

(See also: "Industrial Release Placements")

Dependant on the location and needs of the business, collaboration with colleges has many advantages. At a local level this may involve a nearby college of further education and technology, a polytechnic with relevant programmes or a university. The business may be interested on a national basis with collaboration and liaison with other colleges offering specific courses relevant to the hotel, catering, leisure and tourism industries. A need for fluency in languages in an international organisation, for example, may require close contact with the many hotel and catering schools across Europe.

Whatever the particular needs of the business, consider the points below as means of improving industry-education cooperation.

(a) Ascertain full details of the courses offered, the types of students and the methods of learning and of gaining practical experience.

(b) Develop a close relationship with a specific tutor, perhaps the Head of Department or an industrial placement tutor.

(c) Visit the college if possible, become familiar with all aspects and become known.

(d) Consider invitations to talk or make presentations to students and tutors, or attend prize-givings and other functions.

(e) Use the college as a possible source of labour — for example casual or part-time work for students.

(f) Make sure the college has relevant literature about the firm.

(g) Establish the possibility of industrial release placements.

(h) Establish links for day-release training of employees (eg HCIMA or City and Guilds qualifications).

(i) Be involved in college forums, such as industrial advisory committees, where it is possible to influence course content and development.

(j) It is also possible to be involved on judging panels for student project presentations, or even to be an external examiner, assisting in the monitoring of results and standards of student work.

(k) The college could be an informal or formal source of information, advice and assistance. Some colleges will act as consultants if required.

(l) A pressing problem could be solved by giving a project to the college for a group of students to tackle.

(m) Return or intitiate an invitation to the college tutor and students to visit the business, for a familiarisation talk or a tour, or possibly a work-shadowing experience.

(n) 1991 saw the formation of a group of leading hospitality-oriented polytechnics in the Hospitality Management Learning Consortium. By pooling their resources of experience and knowledge in education and training, their aim is to develop further their links with industry, and to provide specialist services such as the assessment of prior learning and the accreditation of in-company training programmes. The colleges involved are:

(i) Brighton Polytechnic

(ii) Oxford Polytechnic

(iii) Manchester Polytechnic

(iv) Napier Polytechnic.

(See Appendix 3 for addresses.)

COMPETITORS

(See also: "Collaboration")

Many hospitality units in one particular locale or area are affected by similar human resource problems, have many similar needs and may consider similar action to overcome employment and training challenges. On an individual basis, small businesses may not have the resources to tackle far-reaching problems. Within the human resource management field, there are many ways in which mutual assistance and collaboration may effect a better outcome for all concerned.

By developing professional respect and trust, the power of synergy can achieve tremendous results. This does not negate the beneficial influences of competition, but encourages even more improvement and effort to make each business more successful, particularly in beating other industries in attracting and keeping staff.

Consider the following approaches, and review where the business stands with human resource competitors and colleagues:

(a) Meet and build relationships on a constructive and positive basis with local managers, proprietors and human resource managers.

(b) Join or perhaps initiate a local personnel management association, representing a group of businesses. The aim is to discuss and take collaborative action on the key issues, to share information and to update each other on employment matters, such as the implications of new legislation. The aim is to improve human resource management standards overall, and to ensure that the local area is attractive to employees.

(c) Organise joint recruitment campaigns, sharing costs and time; for example, a recruitment drive in a distant location which is a potential source of labour.

(d) Establish joint training courses, particularly those fulfilling statutory needs, like hygiene and health and safety matters.

(e) Consider the mutual referral of good candidates. With time it should become a two-way process.

(f) Useful surveys and comparisons may be carried out on such subjects as compensation and benefits. (Levels of confidentiality need to be established, of course.)

(g) Joint amenities for employees, such as social and sports events, health care and accommodation

(h) Collaboration in the form of an association, however informal, providing "clout" in dealing with suppliers, enabling preferential discounts on training provision, training equipment, print material and employment agency fees

(i) An association which gives a stronger voice when addressing human resource issues with external organisations such as the Job Centre, local government and TECs

(j) Joint action leading to the setting up of career conventions and open days for schools and colleges

(k) Involvement in other forums where managers and those of competitors may participate (for example, HCIMA branch meetings).

CONSULTANTS

In the last few years there has been a considerable growth in the number of consultants with a specific brief to provide a service to hospitality businesses. They range from individuals, normally ex-industry operators or specialists, to international firms with bases across the globe.

Costs can range from £250 to £800 per day, therefore to engage a consultant is a decision which must be thoroughly assessed. The need to hire an external consultant must be explored fully and clearly identified. Normally, such a step will be necessary due to a major strategic issue, not one of routine tactics. The management must be convinced that it is necessary and that such assistance would add value to the existing, internal management of the organisation.

Why use a consultant?

- A business may not possess the necessary skill, ability or expertise internally to tackle a major challenge. This could include a specific training programme where highly specialised knowledge is required.
- Management may not have the time to solve a particular problem which requires considerable research, investigation and assessment.
- There may be a one-off or temporary requirement, for which the business would not need a long-term full-time appointment (eg recruitment for the opening of a new business).

- It may be necessary to have the benefit of an external and "fresh" pair of eyes to review procedures and systems and make recommendations based on experience and specialised ability.

The process

- Identify the real problem — the causes, not just the symptoms. For example, the symptom may be queues for a breakfast table. The causes could be insufficient tables, poorly trained staff or slow replenishment of the buffet. Only identifying and eradicating the true cause will reduce the queues.
- Has the management team been given enough chance to solve the problem themselves? Do they have the skills and the time?
- What is the financial and quality impact of the issue? This will greatly influence the decision on whether or not to spend more money on putting things right.
- Review the budget, available for consultancy fees and assess the "return" which will be expected from the assignment.
- Choose a consultant with the necessary skills and experience, with clear commitment and within the budget, and with whom one is personally comfortable and impressed.
- When briefing the chosen consultant be prepared with all the necessary information, clearly defined objectives and targeted outcomes.
- Establish an agreed process with the consultant, including the method of working, levels of confidentiality, the internal personnel to be involved, the communication, review and feedback systems. A full proposal and time plan must be obtained from the consultant at an early stage in the process.

How to contact consultancy services

A directory of consultants involved in the hospitality industry is obtainable from the Hotel, Catering and Institutional Management Association (HCIMA) (see Appendix 3). This list is also published in the annual *HCIMA Reference Book*.

Many colleges, polytechnics and universities provide consultancy services, so it may be useful to contact a local institution or another prominent college which has a specialist hospitality department.

EMPLOYMENT AGENCIES

There are many registered employment agencies which deal exclusively with hotel and catering staff. Others include hospitality workers as a significant part of their business. Some often concentrate on temporary or casual employees and operative level staff, while others specialise in management and more senior or specialist appointments. A business will pay a considerable fee if an employee is recruited through this method and therefore the need to use an agency must be clearly established.

It should also be remembered that the Job Centre is a free alternative for many grades of staff.

As a potential fee-paying client of an agency, the human resource manager must be in the driving seat, and ensure that he or she gets the service required for the business.

1. Ensure that senior managers and line management agree a clear policy on the use of any employment agency, including the grades of staff involved, the contact procedure, terms and conditions, training to be provided, and that they know the costs involved.
2. Select an agency with experience and a track record in hospitality; get opinions from colleagues in other units.
3. Establish close, clear links with an agency, getting to know an individual at the agency personally. Meet the agency recruiter at one's own business premises.
4. Obtain and understand the agency's terms for recruiting staff of all grades:
   (a) the fee structure
   (b) the procedure for return of the fee if a recruit leaves soon after appointment
   (c) the system of pre-selection
   (d) how the agency communicates with the business
   (e) how candidate data is presented
   (f) the billing procedure.
5. Be assertive about how the service should operate.
6. The agency recruiter must get to know the business establishment thoroughly, its overall standards, the type of employees required, the training, benefits and uniform offered and the social skills required. This will avoid unnecessary time wasted on unsuitable candidates.

7. Be fair to the agency recruiter by giving clear instructions on the requirements for a particular vacancy. A detailed specification should be given, which will save time in the long run.
8. Be particularly careful regarding temporary, casual workers; the quality of the product and customer service can be reduced drastically by the employment of low quality, untrained "agency staff". Be sure that the unit's procedure does not allow a panic-stricken supervisor to contact the agency direct and obtain the costly services of a totally unsuitable worker.

Code of practice

The Federation of Recruitment and Employment Services Limited (FRES) is the recognised trade association for employment agencies with over 3000 offices in membership (address in Appendix 3). It has produced a useful leaflet. *Choosing a Specialist Hotel and Catering Recruitment Service*, and has published the Hotel Catering and Leisure Section's Code of Practice which is reproduced below.

Permanent placements

- Members shall not submit a candidate's details to a client without the candidate's specific knowledge and agreement.
- Members shall not submit a candidate unless adequate steps have been taken to ensure that the candidate meets the client's requirements.
- Members shall ensure that a candidate is in possession of relevant facts and information about the employment before submitting the candidate.
- Members shall not take up a reference from a candidate's current employer without the candidate's authority.
- Members shall not deliberately attempt to induce any employee to leave his or her employment where the member has previously received a fee for placing him or her in the position, unless the present employer agrees to such an approach.

Temporary Placements

- Members shall interview all temporary workers before engagement.

- Members shall satisfy themselves that the temporary workers meet the client's requirements with regard to skill and expertise.
- Members shall take up references for temporary workers and shall inform their clients of those cases where replies have not been received before the temporary worker commences work.
- In calculating pay rates to temporary workers, members shall have regard to permanent pay rates for comparable work.
- Members shall deduct PAYE income tax, and National Insurance in accordance with s.134 of the Income and Corporation Taxes Act 1988.
- Members shall ensure that workers have valid work permits if they do not hold a British passport or relevant EC passport prior to commencing work.

HCIMA

The Hotel, Catering and Institutional Management Association (HCIMA) is the professional body of the hospitality industry. Its remit is to define and maintain the standards of hospitality management education, experience and practice which will ensure the success and development of the industry and its members. Its stated primary objectives are:

(a) The promotion of standards of good practice in catering and accommodation management.
(b) The advancement of education and training and the promotion of research.

Membership is obtained through experience and qualification, full details of which may be obtained direct from the HCIMA (see Appendix 3). For many managers without a formal higher education qualification, such as a degree or diploma, membership may be studied for at many colleges throughout the country, often on a day-release basis, firstly to certificate and then to professional diploma level. Managers should be encouraged and given appropriate support to become members of this industry-wide organisation.

From its base in London, the full-time staff of the Association provide members with some extremely valuable services:

(a) an information office and library which responds to personal, written and telephone enquiries on most conceivable topics
(b) a monthly publication, *Hospitality*, with news, articles and updating information
(c) an appointments service through approved agencies
(d) a book service, bibliography and student reading lists
(e) a financial and business advisory service
(f) a legal advisory and employment issues advisory service
(g) an advisory service with respect to members' own personal career development
(h) a technical advisory group.

HCIMA branches

Human resource managers should make an effort to be involved with the HCIMA branch serving their area. The committees are made up of senior operators, specialists and academics, and arrange a regular series of events, both informative and social. Members and student members are welcome at all events, and full and active participation is very rewarding, both professionally and socially.

INSTITUTE OF PERSONNEL MANAGEMENT

The IPM is firmly established and recognised as an influential and powerful professional body for personnel managers. Its President, Mr Barry Curnow, described the IPM in the 1990 Annual Report, as "the leading organisation in the development of human resource management and promotion of best practice". Membership of the institute, through qualification and experience, is a prized status, and many colleges throughout the country offer a variety of courses and learning methods towards the necessary qualification. A considerable number of hospitality firms are supporting and encouraging personnel specialists to take this route, often beginning with the Certificate in Personnel Practices.

However, throughout the hotel and catering industry, there are still relatively few corporate members.

The IPM offers members a wide range of advisory and information services, including publications and training courses, and full details may be obtained direct (see Appendix 3 for the address).

Participation in IPM branch events should stimulate a wider view of human resource management, and we can always learn from other industries just as other industries can learn from our own.

JOB CENTRES

Job Centres are a most important source of labour throughout the country and are developing improved services under the direction of the Employment Department Group. The Employment Service, the agency of the Group, was created in 1987 with the specific aim of positively assisting the unemployed to find a job. As a result, Job Centres are assuming a wider range of responsibilities and offering a more professional service to the unemployed and the searching employer. They are gradually absorbing much of the work of the unemployment benefit offices, and the intention is that by the mid-1990s the entire service will be under one roof, still to be called Job Centres.

Employers must be fully aware of how to use the local Job Centre; most of the services are free of charge.

Job Centre services

- A free job finding agency, working in liaison with local employers for all grades of vacancy.
- An executive and professional service for more senior jobs on a national network basis.
- Advice and practical guidance to the unemployed on how best to go about getting a job.
- Implementation of government employment schemes.
- Financial help regarding interview preparation and travel expenses.
- Job search seminars for those unemployed for three months or more.
- Job review workshops to consider career options for executive, professional and administrative candidates.

- Jobclub service, offering coaching on job hunting and help with interviewee skills, travel and associated expenses such as telephone calls, stationery and stamps.
- Job Interview Guarantee (JIG) Scheme, whereby the longer-term unemployed are matched to suitable employers, prepared for the type of work and guaranteed an interview (see below).
- "Restart" scheme and courses, providing advice and help to those unemployed for six months or more.
- Specialist help for people with disabilities via the Disablement Advisory Service and its Disablement Resettlement Officers.
- Basic skills training and English language tuition for speakers of other languages.
- A range of training facilities and provision including training for young people towards a vocational qualification, adult training, work trials, open learning and career development.

The Job Interview Guarantee Scheme

This recently introduced scheme is of particular interest to employers, both in small and large organisations. By agreeing at least to interview the candidates specially selected by the Job Centre, employers can receive a far more structured service and be physically involved in the preparation process if desired. The scheme includes:

- job preparation courses: potential candidates are specifically coached towards vacancies over five days, and the employer can make presentations about the firm and the possible jobs. These courses are paid for by the Employment Service.
- work trials, whereby the business can give potential employees a trial of between one and 15 days on the job, unpaid, while they still receive benefit, plus travel and meal expenses. The firm must interview at the end of the trial period, or sooner if things work out well
- there is the opportunity to "adopt" a Jobclub, giving talks and assistance to the members, eventually interviewing those interested in a vacancy placed with the club
- customised training may be arranged to satisfy particular job skill needs. Again, the firm would need to interview any person reaching the required standard as a result of this training.

There is much more to the average local Job Centre than the simple redirecting of the unemployed to any reported vacancy. The past has seen considerable frustration between Job Centres and hospitality firms, leading to charges of unsuitable candidates, wasted time and a lack of understanding on both sides. It is necessary to develop a strong relationship with the local Job Centre, working in cooperation for mutual benefit.

Meet the people at the Job Centre, make a presentation about your business and its labour needs, and invite them to the unit to gain a better insight into your requirements.

When registering a vacancy, give as much information as possible with a clear, precise specification, and keep in touch with the Job Centre to review progress and to report a satisfactory conclusion.

SCHOOLS

Schools of all types should be seen as a good potential source of both employees and customers. The sooner they are aware of the hospitality business the better. Yet the significance of the industry needs constant and positive reinforcement. Many careers teachers and parents have traditionally had a poor image of hotels and catering outlets as employers. They are therefore an unhelpful influence on children when addressing the crucial issues of career options.

Recently there has been an encouraging trend for these groups to realise the importance of the sector and its growth potential. The whole area of leisure and tourism-related business is therefore increasingly being seen as an attractive career and job provider. There have been a number of factors which have affected the attitude of schools:

(a) better links between the industry and schools via "Compacts", career conventions and teacher work-placements
(b) high profile nationwide campaigns by leading employers, giving positive information and advice to youngsters
(c) a GCSE in travel and tourism is now established as an option on the National Curriculum, including short periods of work experience for 14 and 15-year-olds.

Local action

(a) Visit local schools and meet the appropriate careers teachers. Include schools for special needs students, many of whom could be given excellent opportunities to contribute to a hospitality business.
(b) Be prepared to give talks and presentations in the schools. Give them literature and posters for their careers rooms.
(c) Offer teacher placements, such as one week's shadowing. Many towns have a teacher placement service, run by the local authority or the Training and Enterprise Council.
(d) Offer work experience placements for the schoolchildren.
(e) Organise an open day for children, their teachers and parents to gain more insight into the business.
(f) Be prepared to show groups of children around the unit.
(g) Some businesses arrange a tea-party and give the children an appropriate gift.

Much of this activity will only reap benefits in the longer term, but it is vital to think in longer strategic timespans, particularly with the number of school leavers continuing to fall well into the 1990s. A positive experience of the hospitality business at an early age can strongly influence the future choice of education, training and job preferences.

SOCIAL CHARTER

There has been, and will continue to be, much discussion and debate over the European Single Market which is effective from 1 January 1993. Many of the implications are unclear but its relevance should not be dismissed and all employers and managers of people should acquire some level of understanding of its main proposals and philosophies.

With specific regard to employment, the Social Charter is exercising the minds of business people, human resource managers and politicians, and it is important for hospitality managers to be aware of the aspects of the Charter which would have major effects on the business if fully implemented.

One thing is clear, there will undoubtedly be more, not less, employment legislation. Our European partners already possess more statutory provisions as, unlike the United Kingdom, they do not have the foundation of common law to settle many disputes.

The present Conservative Government and most leading employers are highly critical of some of the Social Charter proposals, believing them to be too prescriptive and legislative, and fearing the enormous cost increases that would result. Many point out the irony that in aiming to improve the conditions of work of all employees, the outcome would be less jobs and more redundancies. The hospitality industry would be particularly affected by the following intentions:

(a) To upgrade the rights of part-time and temporary workers to the level of full-time employees, providing equality of treatment, reducing differences in law and practice, and giving them equal health and safety protection.

(b) To specify maximum hours to be worked, which are likely to be rigid and relatively low, in an effort to avoid hours and patterns of work which could be detrimental to employees' health.

(c) To make maternity rights available to more women, with no qualifying period (ie removing the two years' service requirement in United Kingdom law), and with more maternity leave on full pay.

(d) All workers to receive a written statement of employment within one month.

(e) Further legislation would endorse and strengthen existing arrangements on equal opportunities and pay, information and consultation with employees, worker participation and training.

(f) There are clauses affecting rest periods, night shifts and overtime.

TRAINING AND ENTERPRISE COUNCILS

Training and Enterprise Councils (TECs) or Local Enterprise Councils (LECs) in Scotland are being set up throughout the country in an attempt to tackle training issues more effectively and help businesses to be more successful. In all, it is planned that there will be 82 Councils, with local employers very much the driving force behind them. At the time of writing, TECs are mostly in their infancy, but it is likely that employers small and large will have some dealings and contact with some aspect of their work before too long.

The hospitality industry is beginning to get involved. The British Hospitality Association is actively submitting the names of leading executives to be board members, and the Hotel and Catering Training Company (HCTC) is monitoring training standards for the TECs as far as the hospitality business is concerned.

In regions where tourism and hospitality is a key industry, considerable progress has been made. For example, the Devon and Cornwall TEC is piloting a Training Credits Scheme whereby some 40,000 16 to 17-year-olds will receive vouchers of up to £1500 to put towards training of their choice.

The following list shows that TECs are getting involved in some significant areas: employment schemes like Youth Training and the Government's Employment Action programme being promoted through Job Centres.

TEC responsibilities

- To ensure delivery of national training schemes, including Youth Training (YT), Employment Training (ET) and the Enterprise Scheme for new businesses.
- Assisting the Employment Action programme, notably the scheme for temporary work for the longer-term unemployed (over six months).
- To provide smaller, medium-sized, and new businesses with advice, information and discretionary allowances for business start-ups.
- To provide information on training providers in the area with special emphasis on job skills.
- To promote work experience for young people.
- To develop the teacher placement service in exchanges with local employers.
- To organise management training and development schemes appropriate to their region's needs.

Appendix 1
FURTHER READING AND REFERENCE

Croner's Catering.

Croner's Personnel in Practice.

Boella M., Human Resource Management in the Hospitality Industry (Hutchinson Education) 5th edition Stanley Thornes.

Tyson S. and Fell A., Evaluating the Personnel Function. Hutchinson Education.

Honey P., Improve Your People Skills. IPM.

Jones P. and Merricks P., The Management of Catering Operations. Holt, Rinehart, Winston.

Employee Relations. Hotel and Catering Training Company. ACAS booklets.

Appendix 2
PERSONNEL RECORDS PRO FORMAS

PERSONNEL REQUISITION

Position .... Date required ....

Department .... Replacement .... Perm/Temp .... No hours ....

In budget .... New Position ....

Reason required (to be completed in all cases)

....

....

....

If new position attach job description and person specification.

Department Head ....

Personnel & Training Manager ....

General Manager ....

APPLICATION FORM
CONFIDENTIAL APPLICATION FOR EMPLOYMENT

1. Position applied for: _____

   Available to take up employment (date) _____ Wage/salary required £ _____ pw/m

2. Prepared to work:

   Full time ☐   Part time ☐   Shift work ☐

3. **Personal details**

   Surname _____ Forenames _____

   Address _____

   _____ Post code _____

   Telephone: Private _____ Business _____ Date of birth _____

4. Do you: Own a car? | Yes | No |

   Have a current driving licence?   Provisional ☐   Full ☐   HGV ☐   No ☐

   Have any current endorsements? (give details)

   Are you in good health? | Yes | No | Are there any disabilities which may affect your application? | Yes | No |

   Describe disabilities

   Are you registered disabled? | Yes | No | RDP no. _____

   Do you speak or read a foreign language? | Yes | No | Give details _____

5. **Education**

(Schools attended from age 11)	Dates		Examinations (subjects/results)
	From	To	

6. Further education

Place of education	Dates		Type of training	Qualifications
	From	To		

7. Previous employment (Please include details of your most recent employment here, and use the spaces below to give details of other employments, working backwards from the most recent)

Present/previous employer _____ Type of business _____

Address _____ Starting date _____

_____ Leaving date _____

Starting pay £ _____ per _____ Current/Finishing pay £ _____ per _____

Job title _____

Duties/responsibilities _____

_____

Previous employer _____ Type of business _____

Address _____ Starting date _____

_____ Leaving date _____

Starting pay £ _____ per _____ Finishing pay £ _____ per _____

Job title _____

Duties/responsibilities _____

_____

Previous employer _____ Type of business _____

Address _____ Starting date _____

_____ Leaving date _____

Starting pay £ _____ per _____ Finishing pay £ _____ per _____

Job title _____

Duties/responsibilities _____

_____

Previous employer _____ Type of business _____

Address _____ Starting date _____

_____ Leaving date _____

Starting pay £ _____ per _____ Finishing pay £ _____ per _____

Job title _____

Duties/responsibilities _____

_____

GENERAL

8. Interests/hobbies: (Give details of pastimes, sports, etc)

Offices held in social/sports clubs, etc

9. Public duties (JP, local councillor, etc) undertaken:

10. Have you ever been convicted of a criminal offence? (Declaration subject to the Rehabilitation of Offenders Act):

11. Membership of professional organisation:

12. Do you need a work permit to work in the UK?   Yes | No

13. If offered this position will you continue to work in any other capacity? (give details):

14. Community/volunteer experience

Date	Name and address of organisation	Position/title	Duties
From			
To			

15. Personal referees (not members of your family)

Name _____	Name _____
Address _____	Address _____
_____	_____
Occupation _____	Occupation _____
Telephone no. _____	Telephone no. _____

16. If you wish to do so, please give details of next of kin or person who can be contacted in an emergency.

Name _____

Address _____

Relationship _____

Telephone no. _____ (business) _____ (home)

17. Additional personal details

Applicants are requested to tick the relevant boxes below to enable the company to monitor its equal opportunity policy. Monitoring is recommended by the Codes of Practice for the elimination of racial discrimination and for the elimination of discrimination on the grounds of sex and marital status. This information is used for no other purpose and will be treated as confidential.

Male ☐   Female ☐

Ethnic group:

White ☐   Black-Caribbean ☐   Black-African ☐   Black-other ☐ (please specify) _____

Indian ☐   Pakistani ☐   Bangladeshi ☐   Chinese ☐   Other ☐ (please specify) _____

National Insurance no. ☐☐☐☐☐

18. Recruitment policy

It is the company's policy to employ the best qualified personnel and provide equal opportunity for the advancement of employees including promotion and training and not to discriminate against any person because of race, colour, national origin, sex or marital status.

I authorise the company to obtain references to support this application once an offer has been made and accepted and release the company and referees from any liability caused by giving and receiving information.

Declaration: I confirm that the information given on this form is, to the best of my knowledge, true and complete. Any false statement may be sufficient cause for rejection or, if employed, dismissal.

Signature _____ Date _____

19. For office use only

Starting date _____	NI no. _____ P45 or P46 [Yes] [No]
Job offered _____	Pension entry date _____
Pay _____	References requested _____
Hours of work _____	Driving licence _____ Birth certificate _____
Dept/supervisor _____	Proof of qualifications _____
Payroll no. _____	Union membership _____
Recruitment source _____	

20. Interviewer's use only

Appearance	1	2	3	4	5	Other comments
Communication	1	2	3	4	5	
Experience	1	2	3	4	5	
Intelligence	1	2	3	4	5	Signature (1) _____
Co-operation	1	2	3	4	5	
General impression	1	2	3	4	5	(2) _____

INTERNAL VACANCY APPLICATION FORM

Surname	Forenames	Mr Mrs Miss Ms	Payroll no. Dept.

Instructions: Employees should complete this form and pass it to their immediate superior for signature, before returning the form to Personnel.

Vacancy applied for

Job title _____   Grade _____

Department _____   Closing date _____

Applicant

Present job title _____   Grade _____

Permanent staff [   ]   Temporary staff [   ]   Telephone no/ext. _____

Home telephone no. _____

Qualifications for vacant post

Relevant experience both inside and outside the company

Have you applied for this job before?   Yes [   ]   No [   ]   When?

Employee's signature _____   Date _____

Manager's signature _____   Date _____

Ensure that you have completed all the sections of the form. You may attach a supporting letter if you wish.

RECRUITMENT PROGRESS FORM

Job: _____ Closing date: _____

Advertisement: _____

No.	Name	Date details sent	Application acknowledged	Holding letter	Interview letter	Date of interview	Appointment/ Rejection

INTERVIEW ASSESSMENT

Job applied for: _____ Date: _____

Applicant's name: _____

Interviewer(s): _____

Instructions: Rate the applicant by placing ✓ in appropriate box as soon after the interview as possible.

1. Past employment	2. Skill/knowledge	3. Communication	4. Type of work	5. Written work
☐ Employment pattern unsuitable	☐ Has no knowledge or previous experience of this work	☐ Oral communication of information poor	☐ Not used to this type of work and would not suit	☐ Poor legibility, spelling, grammar
☐ Employment pattern erratic	☐ Has some knowledge or skills relevant to this work	☐ Oral communication of information adequate	☐ Not particularly suited for this work	☐ Legible but many errors
☐ Stable and logical employment pattern	☐ Has knowledge and skills that are relevant to this work	☐ Oral communication good	☐ Generally suited to this type of work	☐ Legible but occasional errors
☐ Past experience and employment pattern is ideally suited to the job and indicates a steady worker	☐ Exceptionally well qualified for this work regarding knowledge/skills	☐ Oral communication exceptionally good	☐ Ideally suited to this work	☐ Exceptionally good legibility and good accuracy

6. Overall impression (standard of dress, attitude, etc.)

☐ Unacceptably poor impression	☐ Acceptable impression	☐ Favourable impression	☐ Excellent impression

7. Will the applicant fit in with other department staff?

Yes ☐ No ☐ Undecided ☐

8. Can the company satisfy the applicant's salary aspirations?

Yes ☐ No ☐

(Any other comments please state overleaf)

9. Are the applicant's qualifications adequate for the job?

Yes ☐ No ☐

10. Is the applicant's journey to work long/difficult?

Yes ☐ No ☐

(Any other comments please state overleaf)

11. Suitability to be offered employment

☐ The applicant is not suited to the work. I would not recommend for employment (Give reasons overleaf)	☐ The applicant might do well in this work but I cannot recommend without reservations (Give reasons overleaf)	☐ The applicant will do well in this kind of work and I would recommend employment	☐ The applicant should be excellent at this job and I would recommend with confidence

Signature _____ Date _____

OFFER LETTER

Dear

Further to your recent interview I am pleased to offer you employment as a   on
the terms detailed below and those set out in the enclosed statement of terms and conditions of employment. This offer is
subject to satisfactory references being obtained, your passing a company medical examination and acceptance of you
by our insurers for the purposes of fidelity bonding.

The following items which were discussed with you at interview and which will apply to this employment are confirmed
as follows:

1. You will be employed by (name of employer) on the company's normal terms and conditions of employment.
2. Your salary will be £   payable monthly in arrears by credit transfer. This will be reviewed
    on
3. Your paid holiday will be based on an annual entitlement of   days plus recognised bank and public holidays.
4. Your hours of work will be based on a normal working week of   hours between
    Monday to Friday. However, due to the nature of this position you may be required to work additional hours should
    this be necessary to fulfil your responsibilities. No extra payments will be made for this additional time.
5. You will be employed initially on a three month probationary period. During this period your employment may be
    terminated with one week's notice on either side. Thereafter the periods of notice to terminate your employment
    are those set out in the enclosed statement of terms.

Should you wish to accept this offer please telephone me immediately in order that we can agree a date of
commencement. You should also complete the attached acceptance slip and return it to me together with the names
and addresses of two work-related referees.

I look forward to hearing from you.

Yours sincerely

Ref:

I hereby accept this offer of employment on the terms detailed above and those contained in the attached statement of
terms and conditions.

Signed _____

Date _____

HEALTH QUESTIONNAIRE

Name: _____ Date of birth: _____

Department: _____ Employee no: _____

Job title: _____ Date of transfer: _____

Please complete this questionnaire. As a result of the information you have given you may be referred to a doctor appointed by the company so that a medical examination can be carried out.

Have you ever:	No	Yes	Please give details
1. Had an operation?			
2. Been seriously injured?			
3. Received in-patient treatment for a physical or mental condition?			
4. Been refused or dismissed from employment for health reasons?			
5. Received a disability pension?			
6. Been registered disabled?			Card no: Expiry date:
7. Been made ill by your work?			
8. Been refused a driver's licence because of ill health?			

Have you suffered from or ever had:

Heart trouble	Yes	No	Lung trouble	Yes	No	Stomach trouble	Yes	No
Skin disease	Yes	No	Eye trouble	Yes	No	Ear trouble	Yes	No

Do you:

Take medicine regularly?	Yes	No	Need glasses to read?	Yes	No	Suffer from any other ailments?	Yes	No

To the best of my knowledge and belief the information given above is correct. I understand that if I am appointed and if the information I have provided is incorrect, I will be liable to dismissal.

Signature: _____ Date: _____

FOOD HANDLER'S DECLARATION

Definition
A Food Handler is a person whose work at any time involves him or her in the handling and/or service of food and drink and the use of equipment and utensils connected with the service and preparation of food and drinks.

NAME ....

DEPARTMENT ....

POSITION ....

I agree to report to my Manager on these ocasions:

1. If I develop an illness involving:

> Vomiting
> Diarrhoea
> Skin Rash
> Septic Skin
> Lesion (Boils, Infected Cuts, etc however small)
> Discharge from ear, eye, nose or any other site

2. Before commencing work following an illness involving any of the above conditions.

3. On return from a trip abroad, during which an attack of vomiting and/or diarrhoea lasted more than 2 days.

4. If another member of my household is suffering from diarrhoea or vomiting.

I confirm that I am not suffering at the present time from any conditions listed above (1) and I have never had Typhoid, paratyphoid or Enteric Fever.

I have read (or had explained to me) and understand the above rules on personnel hygiene.

SIGNATURE: DATE:

WITNESS:

INTERNAL NOTIFICATION OF ENGAGEMENT

Surname	Forenames	Department	Payroll no.

Address	Job title
	Starting date
Tel no.	

Dept /branch/division

Bank account no. _____

Bank sort code _____

Bank name and address _____

_____

Tel ext. no.

NI no. _____

Date of birth _____

Retirement date _____

P/T ☐

F/T ☐

Casual ☐

Temporary ☐

Starting date _____

Job offered _____

Pay _____

Hours of work _____

Dept. supervisor _____

Payroll no. _____

P45 or P46 received | Yes | No |

Pension entry date _____

References requested _____

Driving licence _____ Birth certificate _____

Proof of qualifications _____

Union membership _____

Recruitment source: _____

Routing: Payroll

Records

Head of dept.

227

STATEMENT OF TERMS AND CONDITIONS OF EMPLOYMENT

From (Employer): _____

To (Employee): _____

This statement gives details of your employment with the above named employer and is correct at _____

Continuous Employment

Your employment with this company began on _____

Your continuous employment (taking into account any service
with this company or with a previous employer which counts) began on _____

Job Title

You are employed as:

Pay

Rate of pay/method of calculation:

Pay interval:	Pay Day:	Method of payment:
Shift premium:	Other payments:	

Hours

Normal working hours:

Normal working days:

Meal breaks:	Paid	Unpaid	Working week:	Hours:
Full time	Part time	Shift worker: Yes No		Night worker: Yes No

Overtime

Voluntary: Yes No	Compulsory: Yes No	Guaranteed: Yes No

Rates:

Rules:

Holidays

Holiday year:

Paid public holidays:	Paid annual holiday:
Holiday pay:	Rate of accrual:

Rules and procedure:

228

Sickness Absence

SSP qualifying days:

Company sick pay entitlement:

Rate of payment: _____

Notification and evidence rules: _____

Pensions

A. The company does not operate a pension scheme.

B. The company operates a pension scheme which is:

        Contributory ☐

        Non-contributory ☐

  For full details see:

Your employment is / is not contracted out of the State pension scheme.

Company retirement age:

Notice

From the employer:	From the employee:

Disciplinary Rules

Grievance Procedure

Signed by employee on receipt: _____ Date: _____

PERSONAL HISTORY RECORD

Personal

Surname	Forenames	Clock/Staff no.

Home address	Telephone no.

1st change of address	Telephone no.

2nd change of address	Telephone no.

Sex	Date of birth	Nationality	Ethnic origin

Marital status	No. of children

Emergency contact (name, address, tel.no.)	Relationship

Employment

Work address	Telephone no.

1st change of address	Telephone no.

2nd change of address	Telephone no.

Start date	Work permit	Expiry date

Job History

Date	Dept.	Job title	Reason for change

Terms and Conditions

PT/FT	Temp./Perm.	Working hours	Shift pattern	Hours pw

Holiday entitlement	Co. sick pay entitlement	SSP qualifying days	Pension

Other

Pay History

Date	Current salary	Increase	Remarks

Payroll

Payroll no.	NI no.	Tax code

Bank (name and address)	Bank sort code
	Account no.

230

Health

RDP	Disability		RDP no.
Medical restrictions			

Pension Scheme/Insurance, etc

Date	Comments		Date	Comments

Skills and Qualifications

Educational achievements	
Work qualifications	
Languages and proficiency	Test scores
Other skills	Management experience

Miscellaneous

Professional bodies		
Public offices		Territorial army
Union membership	Check off	Union or safety representative
First aid certificate		Driving licence

Previous Employment

Dates	Company	Position	Reason for leaving	Dates	Company	Position	Reason for leaving

Termination

Due retirement date	Termination date	Termination code

231

INDUCTION CHECKLIST

Name: _____ Department: _____

Job title: _____ Date started: _____

		Tick	Date
1.	Welcome to company	☐	
2.	Confirm name of manager/supervisor	☐	
3.	**Hours:**		
	Clocking-on procedure ☐ Lunch break	☐	
	Flexitime rules ☐ Overtime	☐	
4.	**Holidays:**		
	Entitlement ☐ Payment	☐	
	Authorisation procedure ☐ Holiday booked	☐	
	Other leave ☐		
5.	**Sickness:**		
	Notification procedure ☐ Medical certificates	☐	
	Self certification ☐ Payment	☐	
6.	**Pay:**		
	Basic rate ☐ Day of week/month paid	☐	
	Shift/overtime rate ☐		
	Obtain from employee:		
	P45 or P15/signature on form P46	☐	
	NI number	☐	
	Exemption card (reduced rate NI)	☐	
	Bank details: name, address, account no, sort code	☐	
7.	Notice period either side	☐	
8.	Pension scheme eligibility ☐ Medical insurance	☐	
	Life assurance ☐		
9.	Luncheon voucher arrangements	☐	
	Season ticket loan scheme	☐	
	Discounts available	☐	
	Bonus	☐	

	Tick	Date
10. Give to employee:		
Staff handbook / company rules	☐	
Statement of terms and conditions	☐	
Pension scheme booklet	☐	
House magazine	☐	
Uniform / protective clothing	☐	
Security pass	☐	
11. Obtain from employee:		
Emergency contact: name, address, telephone number	☐	
Sight of driving licence	☐	
12. Explain induction programme	☐	
Any questions?	☐	
13. Introductions in department	☐	
14. Location of services:		
Lavatories	☐	
Restaurant/canteen	☐	
Storage for belongings	☐	
15. Health and safety:		
Policy	☐	
First aid	☐	
Fire/bomb alerts	☐	

Note on new employee to:

Department	☐	Security	☐
Notice boards	☐	Staff magazine	☐

Information to:

Payroll	☐	Pensions	☐

Open personnel file	☐	Record card	☐
Absence card	☐	Clock card	☐
Note in personnel daybook	☐		

Check progress with new employee:

After one week	☐	After three months	☐
After one month	☐		

ITEMISED PAY STATEMENT

Department	Employee no.	Tax week/month

NI no.	NI table	Tax code

Hours	Rate	Bonus/commission/ SSP/SMP	Gross amount
	Total gross pay (A)		

	Amount
Contribution to occupational pension scheme (B)	
Total taxable pay = A-B(C)	

Other deductions		Amount
(i) Tax	(based on C)	
(ii) NI contributions	(based on A)	
(iii)	(based on A)	
(iv)	(based on A)	
(v)	(based on A)	
	Total (D)	

Tax free additions	Amount
(i)	
(ii)	
Total (E)	

Net pay (C−D+E)	

Cumulative amounts		Method of payment
Gross pay		
Net pay		
NI contributions		
Tax		
SSP		
SMP		

Name of employee	Date of payment

JOB DESCRIPTION

---

1. Job title: _____ Grade: _____

Department: _____ Reports to: _____

---

2. Main function of job (NB: In addition to these functions employees are required to carry out such other duties as may reasonably be required)

Liability for cash/stock deficiencies:

---

3. Location

---

4. Supervisory responsibilities / position in structure (Attach outline organisation chart, if appropriate)

---

5. Main duties

Duties/responsibilities (in order of priority)	% of time to be spent	Level of responsibility

---

ACTIVITY PLAN

Name:

Department:

Period of plan:

Activity	What has to be done	Result desired	Who is involved	By when	Final completion date

HOLIDAY PAY AND ENTITLEMENT

Example

Holiday period

The holiday year runs from 1 April to 31 March. Entitlement is calculated on the anniversary date of the start of employment. Requests for holiday must be made well in advance to the immediate supervisor. Holidays cannot be carried over into the next holiday year, and no payment will be made for any outstanding holiday entitlement.

Holiday entitlement

Entitlement to paid holiday is according to the format below, based on length of service and calculated from 1 April following the date of start of employment.

LENGTH OF SERVICE	NO. OF WEEKS	NO. OF WORKING DAYS
1 year	4 weeks	20
1-5 years	4 weeks 2 days	22
5 years plus	4 weeks 4 days	24

Holiday entitlement during and on leaving employment

Entitlement to holidays on starting and during employment, and holiday pay on termination are calculated on the scale below:

MONTH OF STARTING OR TERMINATION	EMPLOYEE STARTING: DAYS TO BE TAKEN BY END OF HOLIDAY YEAR (31 MARCH)			EMPLOYEE LEAVING: DAYS TO BE PAID FROM LAST 1 APRIL		
	Holiday entitlement			Holiday pay		
	20	22	24	20	22	24
April	20	22	24	1	2	2
May	18	20	21	2	3	3
June	16	18	20	3	5	5
July	14	16	18	5	8	8
August	12	14	16	7	10	10
September	11	12	14	9	11	12
October	9	11	12	11	12	14
November	7	10	10	12	14	16
December	5	8	8	14	16	18
January	3	5	5	16	18	20
February	2	3	3	18	20	21
March	1	2	2	20	22	24

Holiday Pay

A day's holiday pay is calculated by dividing your annual salary by 260 (annual working days) to give the rate of pay per working day. Bonuses and overtime will not be included, nor will any expenses. Holiday already taken will be deducted from holiday payments on termination. An employee dismissed for gross misconduct loses any rights to holiday pay. When you work a bank or public holiday, you will be paid at double time with a day off in lieu of the public holiday worked.

SICKNESS
SELF-CERTIFICATION FORM

Part 1
To be completed by Department Head/Supervisor on the first day of absence.

Name .... Department ....

First day of absence .... Expected date of return ....

Date absence notified .... Time .... By whom ....

Stated reason for absence ....

Part 2
To be completed by employee

I certify that I was absent from .... to ....

because ....

If during your period of absence you consulted your doctor please give the doctor's name and address and date of the consultation

....

....

If this absence was in excess of seven calendar days a doctor's certificate should be attached.

My absence was/was not of an industrial origin.

I understand that failure to complete this form honestly will render myself liable to disciplinary action which could lead to dismissal and possible prosecution from the department of Health and Social Security.

Signed .... Date ....

Part 3
To be completed by Department Head.

A   I accept the above statement and recommend payment to be made in accordance with the current Terms and Conditions of Employment.

B   I accept the above statement and no payment should be made.

C   I do not accept the above statement and recommend no payment should be made. The employee wishes/does not wish to appeal.

No. hours lost ....

SIGNED BY DEPARTMENT HEAD ....

ABSENCE REQUEST FORM

Surname	Forenames	Dept/branch	Payroll no.

The following time off work is requested:

Period	From	Day	Month	Year		To	Day	Month	Year

If part of day, beginning at [ ] am/pm to [ ] am/pm

		Working day return date	Day	Month	Year

Reason for absence

☐ Annual holiday   ☐ Death of near relative

☐ Jury/witness duty   ☐ Hospital attendance

☐ Territorial Army   ☐ Appointment for doctor, clinic, optician,
                                     dentist, other (please specify below)

☐ Family responsibilities   ☐ Other (please specify below)

To be completed when absence was not approved in advance.

I was absent on (dates): _____

_____

for the following reason: _____

_____

Reason why prior approval was not sought: _____

_____

Employee's signature: _____   Date: _____

Authorisation for time off   With pay; according to entitlement [ ]

                                                    Without pay [ ]

Manager's signature: _____   Date: _____

ABSENCE RECORD

Year: _____

Name: _____   Department: _____

Clock/staff no: _____   Start date: _____

Wk No.	Mon	Tues	Wed	Thur	Fri	Sat	Sun	Summary	Wk No.	Mon	Tues	Wed	Thur	Fri	Sat	Sun

Remarks:

NOTIFICATION OF MATERNITY LEAVE/
RESIGNATION DUE TO PREGNANCY

Surname	Forenames	Department	Payroll no.

Familiarise yourself with the statutory rights relating to maternity leave and maternity pay. (Leaflets can be obtained from the personnel department or the DSS and the Department of Employment.) Complete this form and return it to your supervisor as soon as possible but at least 21 days before starting maternity leave or leaving to have your baby.

This section to be completed by all employees.

1 I wish to confirm that I am taking leave of absence/leaving work* to have my baby.
I will be stopping work on:
(Please attach letter of resignation and notification of termination form where appropriate.)

Day   Month   Year

2 My expected date of confinement is:

Day   Month   Year

3 I enclose a copy of a certificate giving the expected date of my confinement
issued by my Doctor/Midwife*:
This certificate will be returned to you.

Yes   No

This section to be completed only by those employees who are entitled to take maternity leave.

* 4 I wish to confirm my intention to return to work after the birth of my baby
and that I will return within the statutory period of 29 weeks beginning with the week
in which my confinement falls.

* 5 I do not wish to return to work after the birth of my baby.
(Please attach letter of resignation and notification of termination form.)

Signature: _____ Date: _____

If you need further help or explanation, please contact: _____

Please delete as appropriate.

MATERNITY LEAVE

Surname	Forenames	Department	Payroll no.

Thank you for notifying us that you intend to take maternity leave and of your intention *not to/to return to work after the birth of your baby.

If you hold open your right to return to work you must:

1. return to work within the statutory period allowed (within the period of 29 weeks beginning with the week in which your confinement falls); and

2. write to us at least 21 days before the date you intend to return, giving us the precise date that you will start work again. (You may use the tear off slip below if you wish.)

We will write to you again no earlier than 49 days after your expected week of confinement to check whether you still wish to return to work. You *must reply* to that letter within 14 days of receiving it or you will lose the right to return.

Signature: _____   Date: _____

*Delete as appropriate

- -

Exercising the Right to Return to Work after Maternity Leave

To:	From:

I write to confirm that I shall be returning to work on the date below after taking maternity leave.

Signature: _____   Date: _____

(This notification must be returned no later than 21 days before the date notified above and should be sent to your manager.)

243

CONFIRMATION OF INTENTION TO RETURN TO WORK
FOLLOWING MATERNITY LEAVE

To:	From:

A. When notifying us of your intention to take maternity leave, you indicated that you wished to return to work after the birth of your baby. As you are aware, this must be before the expiry of the statutory period of 29 weeks.

We are now writing to enquire whether or not you still intend to return to work.

Please send confirmation of this intention to us within 14 days of receipt of this correspondence or, if this is not possible, as soon as reasonably practicable. Failure to do this will lose you the right to return to work. You may use part C of this form for the purpose. Part B can be used to notify the actual date of return.

Signature: _____   Date: _____

- -

B.   **Exercising the Right to Return to Work after Maternity Leave**

To:	From:

I write to confirm that I shall be returning to work on the date below after taking maternity leave.

Signature: _____   Date: _____

(This notification must be returned not later than 21 days before the date above, and should be sent to your manager.)

- -

C.   **Reply to Maternity Leave Confirmation Form**

To:	From:

*[1] I wish to confirm my intention to return to work after my maternity leave and my date of return *is given below/ will be sent to you in due course.

*[2] I do not wish to return to work after my maternity leave.

Signature: _____   Date: _____

*Delete as appropriate

ACCIDENT LOG

Name: _____ Clock/staff no: _____

Home address: _____ Department: _____

_____ Job title: _____

_____ Age: _____ Sex: _____

Time and date of accident: _____

Precise location: _____

How did the accident happen?

Names of witnesses: | Clock/staff nos:

Details of apparent injuries:

What immediate action was taken?

Reasons given for cause of accident:

(a) By injured employee | (b) By witnesses

At the time of the accident:

		Yes	No
(a)	Should employee have been on premises?	Yes	No
(b)	Was he/she carrying out normal duties?	Yes	No
(c)	Was he/she acting in accordance with rules?	Yes	No
(d)	Was protective clothing provided for work being done?	Yes	No
(e)	Was it being used?	Yes	No

If the answer to any of these questions is no, provide details on a separate sheet.

Is employee able to continue work?	Yes	No	Date work resumed

Recommendations:

Signature _____

Title _____ Date _____

To be completed by the personnel department

Health and Safety Executive informed by _____ on _____

Insurance company informed by _____

WARNING LETTER

Name: _____ Clock/staff no: _____

Department: _____ Job title: _____

Reason for disciplinary action (give details):

Investigation carried out by: _____

Details of warning:

Level of warning: _____

If no/insufficient improvement by: _____

the next stage will be: _____

This warning will remain active for a period of _____

Disciplinary interview conducted and warning given

by: _____

on: _____

Right of appeal exercised: Yes/No

*Signature: _____ Signature: _____
    For the employer   Employee

Date: _____ Date: _____

Result of appeal: Warning confirmed / deleted / substituted (specify details below)

*The warning should be signed by the person who conducted the disciplinary interview wherever possible.

246

NOTIFICATION OF TERMINATION

Name: _____ Clock/staff no: _____

Department: _____ Location: _____

Job title: _____ Salary: _____

Start date: _____ Termination date: _____

Holiday taken to date: _____ days Period of notice to be worked: _____ weeks

Accrued holiday pay due | Yes | No | Pay in lieu of notice due | Yes | No |

Replacement required: | Yes | No | Employment requisition form   attached [ ]   to follow [ ]

A: Resignation [ ]   Date notice given _____

Written resignation attached: [ ]   Resignation accepted (copy attached): [ ]

or

The following to be completed by the employee and supervisor:

I hereby give notice that I will terminate my employment with the company on _____

Signature _____   Date _____
        Employee

Resignation accepted:

Signature _____   Date _____
        For the company

Reason for resignation if known:

B: Dismissal [ ]   Date notice given _____

Reason for dismissal: | Give details:

  Gross misconduct [ ]

  After warnings [ ]

  Other [ ]

Dismissal confirmed in writing (copy attached): [ ]

C: Retirement [ ] | Completed by:
                         |
D: Death [ ] | Title
                         | Date

CHECKLIST ON TERMINATION

SECTION A To be completed by Departmental Manager only when the employee has completed all duties.

NAME: ....

DEPT: ....

LIVE IN/OUT: ....

TERMINATION DATE: ....

THIS CONFIRMS THAT THE ABOVE EMPLOYEE HAS COMPLETED ALL HIS/HER DUTIES

SIGN. OF DEPT. MANAGER: ....

DATE: ....

SECTION B This confirms that all Uniforms issued have been returned.

SIGNATURE: ....

DATE: ....

NB. If any items are not returned or are returned damaged, this section will not be completed and employee will be referred to Personnel.

SECTION C To be completed by the Personnel Department.

LOCKER KEY RETURNED: YES/NO   CAR PARK PASS: YES/NO

I.D. BADGE: YES/NO

NAME BADGE: YES/NO

To be signed by Personnel: ....

SECTION D   Live in Staff Only – Completed by Personnel

KEYS RETURNED: YES/NO   FORWARDING ADDRESS:

FLAT IN ORDER: YES/NO

DEPOSIT TO BE
RETURNED: YES/NO

SECTION E To be completed by Personnel & Training Manager

(* To be deleted as appropriate)

AUTHORISATION TO PAY FINAL WAGES*

AUTHORISATION TO PASS FINAL WAGES TO HEAD OF DEPARTMENT*

SIGNATURE: .... DATE: ....

LEAVER'S FORM

Name .... Department ....

Job title .... Resignation/dismissal ....

Date effective .... Last working day ....

Outstanding payments

No. holiday .... No lieu day .... other ....

Accom. deposit .... Loan outstanding ....

REASON FOR LEAVING ....

....

Reference – for use by the Personnel Dept. for new employers.

Date of start .... Date of finish .... Length ....

	excellent	good	average	poor
ability				
industriousness				
attendance				
timekeeping				
attitude				

General comment ....

....

....

Re-employ   yes/no

Department Head ....

Personnel and Training Manager ....

General Manager ....

TERMINATION INTERVIEW

Please read a complete this form in full. So that this form can be of use, answer the questions honestly, all information given will be in the strictest of confidence.

NAME: ....

DEPARTMENT: ....

What were your expectations of the firm before you joined?

....
....
....
....
....

Were these expectations met, if so how?

....
....
....

If not explain:

....
....
....

What are your reasons for leaving?

....
....
....

Would you re-join the firm?

....
....
....
....
....

Appendix 3
DIRECTORY OF ORGANISATIONS

Advisory, Conciliation and Arbitration Service (ACAS)
Head Office
27 Wilton Street
London SW1X 7AZ
Tel. 071-210 3000

Regional Offices
Newcastle-upon-Tyne:
  Tel. 091-261 2191
Leeds: *Tel.* 0532 431371
Fleet: *Tel.* 0252 811868
London: *Tel.* 071-388 5100
Bristol: *Tel.* 0272 744066
Birmingham: *Tel.* 021-622 5050
Manchester: *Tel.* 061-228 3222
Glasgow: *Tel.* 041-204 2677
Cardiff: *Tel.* 0222 762636

AIDS
National Aids Helpline
Tel. 0800 555777 (literature)
Tel. 0800 567123 (advice)

Terence Higgins Trust
BM/AIDS
London WC1N 3XX
Tel. 071-833 2971

British Hospitality Association (BHA)
40 Duke Street
London W1M 6HR
Tel. 071-499 6641

British Association of Counselling
37a Sheep Street, Rugby
Warwickshire CV21 3BX
Tel. 0788 78328/9

British Standards Institute (BSI)
2 Park Street
London W1A 2BS
Tel. 071-629 9000

Commission for Racial Equality
Elliot House
10-12 Allington Street
London SW1E 5EH
Tel. 071-828 7022

Data Protection Registrar
Springfield House
Water Lane
Wilmslow
Cheshire SK9 5AX
Tel. 0625 535777

Department of Employment
Caxton House
Tothill Street
London SW1H 9NA
Tel. 071-213 3000

Dyslexia Association
Tonbridge, Kent
Tel. 0732 352762

Equal Opportunities Commission (EOC)
Overseas House, Quay Street
Manchester M3 3HN
Tel. 061-833 9244

HCIMA
191-193 Trinity Road
London SW17 7HN
Tel. 081-672-4251

Health and Safety Executive (HSE)
Baynards House, 1 Chepstow Place
Westbourne Grove
London W2 4TF
Tel. 071-229 3456

Health Education Authority (HEA)
Hamilton House
Mableden Place
London WC1H 1TX
Tel. 071-383 3833

Holiday Care Service
2 Old Bank Chambers
Station Road, Horley
Surrey RH6 9HW
Tel. 0293 774535

Hotel and Catering Training Company
International House
High Street, Ealing
London W5 5DB
Tel. 081-579 2400

Hospitality Management Learning Consortium
Brighton Polytechnic
Department of Service Sector Management
49 Darley Road, Eastbourne
East Sussex BN20 7UR
Tel. 0273 643631

Oxford Polytechnic
Department of Hotel and Catering Management
Gipsy Lane
Headington, Oxford
Tel. 0865 741111

Manchester Polytechnic
Hollings Facility
Department of Hotel Catering and Tourism Management
Old Hall Lane
Manchester
Tel. 061-257 3024

Napier Polytechnic
Department of Hotel and Catering Studies
10 Colinton Road
Edinburgh EH10 5DT

Institute of Manpower Studies
Mantell Building
Brighton BN1 1ZX

Institute of Personnel Management (IPM)
IPM House
35 Camp Road
Wimbledon SW19 4UX
Tel. 081-946 9100

National Association of Pre-menstrual Syndrome (PMS)
PO Box 72
Sevenoaks
Kent TN13 1XQ

Training and Enterprise Council
See local telephone directory

Working Mothers Association
77 Holloway Road
London N17 8JZ

INDEX

management, 186
physical symptoms, 185
Succession planning, 39-40, 109-11
  chart example, 110-11
Supervisor training, 112-13
  checklist, 113
Supervisory appraisal format, 83-6
Suspension from duty, 48

T

Teacher work-placements, 208, 211
Team role, HR manager, 28-30
Technology, introduction, 11
Telephone,
  enquiries, 14
  image, 14
Temporary lay-off, 171
Temporary workers, rights, 210
Terence Higgins Trust, address and
  telephone number, 141, 251
Termination of contract, 114-18
  hearing, 114-15
  interview, 118
    pro forma, 250 Fig
  notification of, pro forma, 247-8
    Fig
  settlement (ACAS settlement),
    117-18
  types of, 115-16
Terms and conditions of
  employment, 15, 34, 44, 54, 63,
  74, 93, 118-20, 129-30, 140, 171
  changes to, 120
  express terms, 119
  implied terms, 179-80
  statement, pro forma, 228-9 Fig
  written statement, 119-20
Tips, 130
Total quality management (TQM),
  90-1
Tourism, importance to economy,
  xiii
Trade union membership, 161

Trainees, 121-3
  recruitment and selection, 123
  types of, 121-2
Training, xiii, 11, 64
  appraisal interviewers, 87
  example, training restaurant staff
    in wine service, 32-3
  food handlers, 159
  Piggy-back training schemes, 196
  quality service standards, 91
Training courses, with competitors,
  199
Training Credits Scheme, 211
Training and Enterprise Councils
  (TECs), 121, 196-7, 210-11
  responsibilities, 211
Training plans, 124-7
  format, example, 126, 127 Fig
  formulating, 124, 126
  see also Induction; Skills training;
    Trainees
Training sessions, use of video
  cameras and recorders, 32

U

Unfair dismissal, 117, 164
  advice from CAB, 195
  redundancy, 174
Uniforms, 13, 15, 34
Unit labour cost, 88, 90

V

Vacancies, 128
  see also, Recruitment; Labour
    market; Succession planning
Verbal warning, 46, 49
Vomiting, 159

W

Wages, 16, 129-32
  advances on, 130
  collection point, 13
  control, 130-1

deductions, 129
payment by credit transfer, 130
system, example, 131-2
Wages Council minimum wage,
129
see also Pay statement;
Productivity; Rotas; Terms and
conditions
Wages Act 1986, 164
Warning letter, pro forma, 246 Fig
Week or five working days in hand
system, 130
Wills, 144
Women, 186-9
pregnant *see* Maternity;
Pregnancy
retirement age, 188
returning to work, 93
statistics, 187
Word processing, 19-20
Work experience, 121, 122, 162
see also Industrial release

placements
Work permit applications, 79-80
Work trials, 207
Work-related stress, 135, 136
Working hours, maximum, 210
Working Mothers Association, 189
address and telephone number,
252
Workplace nurseries, 188
Wounds, covering, 141
Written disciplinary procedures, 45
Written enquiries, 14
Written statement of employment,
210
Written warnings, 46-7, 49
Wrongful dismissal, 116

Y

Young people, 132-4
Youth Training (YT), 121, 133, 211
Youthscan, 133-4
YTS, 133